ClearRevise®

AQA GCSE
German 8662

Illustrated revision and practice

Foundation and Higher

Lucy Dreznin

Published by
PG Online Limited
The Old Coach House
35 Main Road
Tolpuddle
Dorset
DT2 7EW
United Kingdom

sales@pgonline.co.uk
www.clearrevise.com
www.pgonline.co.uk
2024

PG ONLINE

PREFACE

Absolute clarity! That's the aim.

This is everything you need to ace your exams and beam with pride. Each topic is laid out in a beautifully illustrated format that is clear, approachable and as concise and simple as possible.

We have included worked examination-style questions with answers for each of the four papers. This helps you to understand where marks are coming from and to familiarise yourself with the style of questions you will be asked. There is also a set of exam-style questions at the end of each section for you to practise your responses. You can check your answers against those given at the end of the book.

A full **transcript** and **audio clips** can be downloaded from the **clearrevise.com** website, along with tips on how to approach the listening paper and guidance on marking each of the questions.

ACKNOWLEDGEMENTS

Every effort has been made to trace and acknowledge ownership of copyright. The publisher will be happy to make any future amendments with copyright owners that it has not been possible to contact. The publisher would like to thank the following companies and individuals who granted permission for the use of their images or material in this textbook.

Design and artwork: Jessica Webb / PG Online Ltd

All Sections
Photographic images: © Shutterstock
Rose Monday parade © Yulia Reznikov / Shutterstock.com

First edition 2024 10 9 8 7 6 5 4 3 2 1
A catalogue entry for this book is available from the British Library
ISBN: 978-1-916518-01-8
Contributors: Lucy Dreznin
Editor: Jenny Gwynne

This product is made of material from well-managed FSC®-certified forests and from recycled materials. Printed by Bell and Bain Ltd, Glasgow, UK.

MIX
Paper | Supporting responsible forestry
FSC www.fsc.org FSC® C007785

THE SCIENCE OF REVISION

Illustrations and words

Research has shown that revising with words and pictures doubles the quality of responses by students.[1] This is known as 'dual-coding' because it provides two ways of fetching the information from our brain. The improvement in responses is particularly apparent in students when they are asked to apply their knowledge to different problems. Recall, application and judgement are all specifically and carefully assessed in public examination questions.

Retrieval of information

Retrieval practice encourages students to come up with answers to questions.[2] The closer the question is to one you might see in a real examination, the better. Also, the closer the environment in which a student revises is to the 'examination environment', the better. Students who had a test 2–7 days away did 30% better using retrieval practice than students who simply read, or repeatedly reread material. Students who were expected to teach the content to someone else after their revision period did better still.[3] What was found to be most interesting in other studies is that students using retrieval methods and testing for revision were also more resilient to the introduction of stress.[4]

Ebbinghaus' forgetting curve and spaced learning

Ebbinghaus' 140-year-old study examined the rate at which we forget things over time. The findings still hold true. However, the act of forgetting grammar and vocabulary and relearning them is what cements them into the brain.[5] Spacing out revision is more effective than cramming – we know that, but students should also know that the space between revisiting material should vary depending on how far away the examination is. A cyclical approach is required. An examination 12 months away necessitates revisiting covered material about once a month. A test in 30 days should have topics revisited every 3 days – intervals of roughly a tenth of the time available.[6]

Summary

Students: the more tests and past questions you do, in an environment as close to examination conditions as possible, the better you are likely to perform on the day. If you prefer to listen to music while you revise, listen to songs in German. However, tunes without any lyrics will be far less detrimental to your memory and retention, and silence is most effective.[5] If you choose to study with friends, choose carefully – effort is contagious.[7]

1. Mayer, R. E., & Anderson, R. B. (1991). Animations need narrations: An experimental test of dual-coding hypothesis. *Journal of Education Psychology*, (83)4, 484–490.
2. Roediger III, H. L., & Karpicke, J. D. (2006). Test-enhanced learning: Taking memory tests improves long-term retention. *Psychological Science*, 17(3), 249–255.
3. Nestojko, J., Bui, D., Kornell, N. & Bjork, E. (2014). Expecting to teach enhances learning and organisation of knowledge in free recall of text passages. *Memory and Cognition*, 42(7), 1038–1048.
4. Smith, A. M., Floerke, V. A., & Thomas, A. K. (2016). Retrieval practice protects memory against acute stress. *Science*, 354(6315), 1046–1048.
5. Perham, N., & Currie, H. (2014). Does listening to preferred music improve comprehension performance? *Applied Cognitive Psychology*, 28(2), 279–284.
6. Cepeda, N. J., Vul, E., Rohrer, D., Wixted, J. T. & Pashler, H. (2008). Spacing effects in learning: A temporal ridgeline of optimal retention. *Psychological Science*, 19(11), 1095–1102.
7. Busch, B. & Watson, E. (2019), *The Science of Learning*, 1st ed. Routledge.

CONTENTS

The basics

Theme 1 People and lifestyle

Theme 2 Popular culture

Grammar

Tiers, mark schemes and marking guidance

All of the Higher tier exam practice questions in this book have been marked with an **H** symbol. Foundation level questions have been marked with an **F**. Boundary level questions may have both **F** **H**.

The answers to exam questions should be marked in accordance with the mark schemes published on the AQA website. A set of guidance notes on how to interpret the mark schemes for each question type on each paper can be downloaded from **ClearRevise.com**. This also contains advice and tips on how to gain as many marks as you can.

Understanding the specification reference tabs

This number refers to the Theme number. In this example, **Theme 2: Popular culture**.

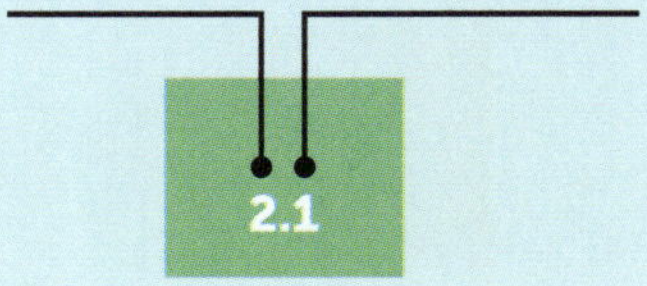

This number refers to the Topic number. In this example, **Topic 1: Free-time activities**.

Downloading the speaking and listening clips

All of the MP3 audio clips can be downloaded from our website at **ClearRevise.com/8662**.

A full copy of the **transcripts** is also available to download.

TRACK 1

Scan the **QR code** here or on each question with a **listening or speaking symbol**.

Then select the **track** indicated.

THE BASICS

No vocabulary is specified for KS2 or KS3 so this section includes some key words and phrases that students at all levels will find helpful. This book makes no assumptions about vocabulary previously taught.

BASIC WORDS AND PHRASES

Die Wochentage — *The days of the week*

Montag	Dienstag	Mittwoch	Donnerstag	Freitag	Samstag	Sonntag
Monday	*Tuesday*	*Wednesday*	*Thursday*	*Friday*	*Saturday*	*Sunday*

! Like English, German capitalises its days of the week. **Every noun in German** starts with a capital letter.

am Wochenende
at the weekend

Useful phrases

am Montag	*on Monday*	montags	*on Mondays*
jeden Montag	*every Monday*	jeden Tag	*every day*
dieses Wochenende	*this weekend*	letzten Samstag	*last Saturday*
nächste Woche	*next week*	letztes Jahr	*last year*
heute	*today*	morgens	*in the mornings*
gestern	*yesterday*	morgen	*tomorrow*
vorgestern	*the day before yesterday*	übermorgen	*the day after tomorrow*
gestern Morgen	*yesterday morning*	morgen Nachmittag	*tomorrow afternoon*
gestern Abend	*last night*	heute Abend	*tonight*
immer	*always*	manchmal	*sometimes*
nie	*never*	oft	*often*

Wie spät ist es? — *What time is it?*

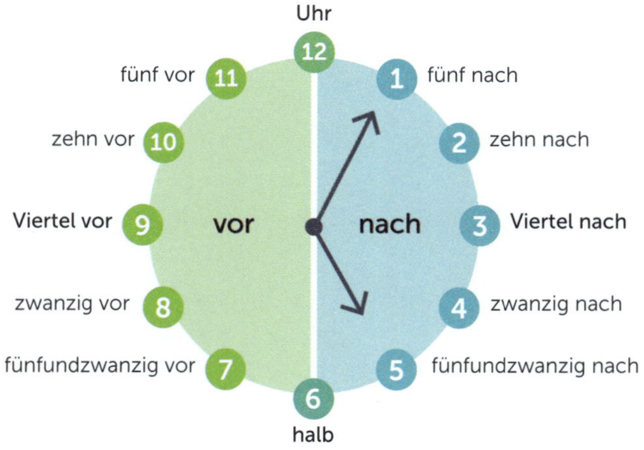

Es ist ... Uhr.
It is ... o'clock.

Es ist zehn Uhr dreizehn.
It is 10:13.

Es ist Viertel nach zehn.
It is quarter past ten.

Es ist Viertel vor elf.
It is quarter to eleven.

Es ist halb elf.
It is half past ten. (Literally, halfway towards eleven o'clock.)

Die Monate und Jahreszeiten | *Months and seasons*

Januar *January*	Februar *February*	März *March*
April *April*	Mai *May*	Juni *June*
Juli *July*	August *August*	September *September*
Oktober *October*	November *November*	Dezember *December*

im Frühling
spring

im Sommer
summer

im Herbst
autumn

im Winter
winter

Mein Geburtstag ist im Januar. — *My birthday is in January.*

Im Sommer gehen wir zum Strand. — *In summer we go to the beach.*

Heute haben wir den 13. (dreizehnten) November. — *Today is the 13th of November.*

Wir machen immer am 1. (ersten) Januar Party. — *We always have a party on the first of January.*

Die Zahlen | *Numbers*

1	eins	**11**	elf	**21**	einundzwanzig	**40**	vierzig
2	zwei	**12**	zwölf	**22**	zweiundzwanzig	**50**	fünfzig
3	drei	**13**	dreizehn	**23**	dreiundzwanzig	**60**	sechzig
4	vier	**14**	vierzehn	**24**	vierundzwanzig	**70**	siebzig
5	fünf	**15**	fünfzehn	**25**	fünfundzwanzig	**80**	achtzig
6	sechs	**16**	sechzehn	**26**	sechsundzwanzig	**90**	neunzig
7	sieben	**17**	siebzehn	**27**	siebenundzwanzig	**100**	(ein)hundert
8	acht	**18**	achtzehn	**28**	achtundzwanzig	**1000**	(ein)tausend
9	neun	**19**	neunzehn	**29**	neunundzwanzig	**100 000**	(ein)hundert-tausend
10	zehn	**20**	zwanzig	**30**	dreißig	**1 000 000**	eine Million

der/die/das erste — *the first*

der/die/das dritte — *the third*

+ To make ordinal numbers (fifth, sixth, etc.), add the endings **-te** or **-ste**. When giving the date, these will often change to **-ten** and **-sten**.

Die Farben — *Colours*

braun	rot	gelb	grün	blau	weiß	grau	schwarz
brown	*red*	*yellow*	*green*	*blue*	*white*	*grey*	*black*

+ You can add **dunkel** (*dark*) or **hell** (*light*) to colours:

Die Socken sind dunkelrot.	*The socks are dark red.*
Der Himmel ist hellblau.	*The sky is light blue.*

Colour endings change when used as an adjective before a noun. The ending depends on the gender of the noun being described and the grammatical case. For more about adjectives, go to **page 12** and **page 140**.

Ich habe dunkelrote Socken.	*I have dark red socks.*
Ich laufe unter dem hellblauen Himmel.	*I run under the light blue sky.*

Greetings and being polite

Guten Tag / Hallo Grüß Gott / Servus	*Hello / Hi*
Guten Abend	*Good evening (used from late afternoon onwards)*
Gute Nacht	*Good night*
Willkommen	*Welcome*
Wie geht's?	*How are you?*
Auf Wiedersehen	*Goodbye*
Viel Glück!	*Good luck!*
Herzlichen Glückwunsch!	*Congratulations!*
bitte	*please*
danke	*thank you*
alles klar	*okay*
Entschuldigung	*sorry/excuse me*
Entschuldigen Sie, bitte	*Excuse me, please*
meine Damen und Herren	*ladies and gentlemen*

Conjunctions

und	*and*
oder	*or*
aber	*but*
denn Ich mag Musik, <u>denn</u> sie <u>ist</u> cool.	*because* *I like music* *because it is cool.*
weil Ich mag Musik, <u>weil</u> sie cool <u>ist</u>.	*because* *I like music* *because it is cool.*

Likes and dislikes

Ich mag ...	*I like ...*
Ich mag ... nicht	*I don't like ...*
Ich liebe ...	*I love ...*
Ich hasse ...	*I hate ...*

Ich + verb + **gern** / **nicht gern** ... *I like / do not like ...*

Ich + verb + **lieber** ... *I prefer ...*

Opinions

You can introduce your opinion with **Ich denke**, **Ich glaube**, **Ich finde** / *think* or **Meiner Meinung nach...** *In my opinion...* Then go on to express your ideas.

TRACK 1

PHONICS

These are the most important sounds in German. Listen to the recording, then have a go yourself.

Letter	Sound	Examples
ä	A narrow vowel sound. Give the 'ay' sound, like in the English word *say*, then narrow the corners of your mouth.	spät, Käse, Bär
au	Like 'ow' in the English word *how.*	laut, faul, Traum
äu	Like 'oy' in the English word *soya.*	häufig, Träume
ch	Like a hard 'h', almost a 'k'. Think of a cat hissing.	ich, sicher, nicht
ei	Like the English word *eye*. Often confused with the **ie** combination in German. The second letter is what makes the correct sound.	Eier, zwei, mein
er	Like 'air' in the English words *air* and *hair.*	er, der
	Like 'ur' in the English word *fur.*	Mutter, Bruder
eu	Like 'oy' in the English word *soya*. Same sound as **äu**.	teuer, treu, Freund
ie	Like 'ee' or 'ea' in the English words *see* or *sea*. Often confused with the **ei** combination in German. The second letter is what makes the correct sound.	sie, Dienstag
j	Like 'y' in the English word *your.*	Jahr, Jugend, jeden
ö	A narrow vowel sound. Give the 'oh' sound in English and then narrow the corners of your mouth.	schön, Österreich
qu	A 'kv' sound.	bequem, Qualität
ß	The sharp 's'. Stands for a double 's', an 'ss' sound. Elongate the 's' sound in a German word with this letter.	heiße, Straße, groß
sch	Like 'sh' in the English word *ship*.	Schwester
sp-	A 'shp' sound when appearing at the start of a word.	Spaß, Sport
st-	A 'sht' sound when appearing at the start of a word.	Stein, still, streng
ü	A narrow vowel sound. Give the 'oo' sound, like in the English word *look,* and then narrow the corners of your mouth.	über, Übung
v	Like 'f' in the English word *feel.*	voll, vier, kreativ
w	Like 'v' in the English word *vase*.	was, warum
z	Like an 's' sound with a very slight 't' in front: 'ts'.	zehn, Zähne

Masculine and feminine nouns for people

Throughout this revision guide, you will see nouns in German referring to people. For example, this could be the word for friend (**der Freund**) or a job title (**der Lehrer** *teacher*, **der Trainer** *trainer*). This is the masculine version of each noun. To talk about a female person, add the letters **-in** to the end of the word: **die Freundin**, **die Lehrerin**, **die Trainerin**. Similarly, when you see the feminine noun form, you can remove the letters **-in** to talk about a male person.

TOPICS FOR THEME 1

People and lifestyle

Specification coverage

Topic 1 Identity and relationships with others

Topic 2 Healthy living and lifestyle

Topic 3 Education and work

Information about the four papers for Foundation F and Higher H tiers:

Paper 1 – Listening

Written exam:
35 minutes F, 45 minutes H
40 marks F, 50 marks H
25% of GCSE

The recording is controlled by the invigilator with built-in repetitions and pauses.

Each exam includes 5 minutes' reading time at the start of the question paper before the listening material is played and 2 minutes at the end of the recording to check your work.

Section A – Listening comprehension questions in English, to be answered in English or non-verbally (F 32 marks, H 40 marks).

Section B – Dictation where students transcribe 4 sentences (F 8 marks) or 5 sentences (H 10 marks).

Paper 3 – Reading

Written exam: 45 minutes F, 1 hour H
50 marks, 25% of GCSE

Section A – Reading comprehension questions in English, to be answered in English or non-verbally (40 marks).

Section B – Translation from German into English, minimum of 35 words F or 50 words H (10 marks).

Paper 2 – Speaking

Non-exam assessment (NEA):
7–9 minutes F or 10–12 minutes H +
15 minutes' supervised preparation time
50 marks, 25% of GCSE

Role play – 10 marks, 1–1.5 minutes. F H

Reading aloud passage and short conversation – 15 marks.
Recommended time 2–2.5 minutes F and 3–3.5 minutes H.
Minimum 35 words F and minimum 50 words H.

Photo card discussion (two photos) – 25 marks.
Photo card discussion time:
4–5 minutes F and 6–7 minutes H.

Paper 4 – Writing

Written exam: 1 hour 10 minutes F,
1 hour 15 minutes H
50 marks, 25% of GCSE

Set of three short writing tasks. F only. 25 marks.

Translation of sentences from English into German, minimum 35 words F, or 50 words H (10 marks).

Produce a piece of writing in response to three compulsory bullet points, approximately 90 words in total. Choose from two questions (15 marks). F H

Open-ended writing task.
Two compulsory bullet points, approximately 150 words in total. Choose from two questions. (25 marks). H only.

INTRODUCTIONS

Mich — *Me*

Here are four questions someone might ask when they want to get to know you.

Wie heißt du?	*What is your name?*
Wo wohnst du?	*Where do you live?*
Wie alt bist du?	*How old are you?*
Wann hast du Geburtstag?	*When is your birthday?*

Remember

Wie? means *how?* So **Wie heißt du?** means literally, *How are you called?*
Wo? means *where?*
Wann? means *when?*
For more details about question words, go to **page 159**.

Your answers to the questions above will usually include the following phrases.

Ich heiße ...	*My name is... / I am called...*
Ich wohne ...	*I live...*
Ich bin ... Jahre alt.	*I am ... years old.*
Ich habe am ... Geburtstag.	*My birthday is on the...*

1. You hear a short interview with a young person from Germany. Select the correct option to complete each sentence.

TRACK 2

1.1	Franz is ...	**A** 16 years old.	**B** 26 years old.	**C** 36 years old.
1.2	Franz lives in ...	**A** Berlin.	**B** Munich.	**C** Cologne.
1.3	Franz's mother ...	**A** comes from Frankfurt.	**B** lives in Frankfurt.	**C** is not German.
1.4	Franz's birthday is on ...	**A** 18th of December.	**B** 28th of December.	**C** 8th of December.

1.1 A 1.2. A 1.3 A 1.4 A

Fragen und Antworten *Questions and answers*

When answering questions about yourself, try and develop your answers.

Here are some examples.

Wie heißt du?

Mein Name ist Franziska, aber Fran ist besser.
My name is Franziska, but Fran is better.

Wo wohnst du?

Ich wohne mit meiner Familie in einem Dorf in der Nähe von Berlin.
I live with my family in a village close to Berlin.

Wie alt bist du?

Ich bin sechzehn Jahre alt und bald werde ich siebzehn.
I am sixteen years old and soon I am going to be seventeen.

Wann hast du Geburtstag?

Ich habe am neunten Januar Geburtstag, aber meine kleine Schwester hat am siebten Geburtstag!
My birthday is on the ninth of January, but my little sister's is on the seventh!

2. How would you answer the four questions above?
Prepare your answers, then listen to the recording and give your response.

TRACK 3

+ Think of extra details you can add. Here are some ideas you can adapt and use.

Mir gefällt mein Name. *I like my name.*	**Es liegt im Norden/Osten/Süden/Westen von ...** *It is in the north/east/south/west of ...*
... aber alle nennen mich ... *... but everyone calls me ...*	**... aber mein Bruder/meine Schwester ist ...** *... but my brother/my sister is ...*
... aber ich komme aus ... *... but I come from ...*	**Ich finde es toll, Geburtstag zu feiern.** *I think it's great to celebrate your birthday.*

PERSONALITY

Meine Familie, Freunde und ich — *My family, friends and I*

meine Familie *my family*			
mein Vater *my father*	mein Bruder *my brother*	mein Halbbruder *my half-brother*	mein Onkel *my uncle*
mein Stiefvater *my stepfather*	mein Stiefbruder *my stepbrother*	meine Halbschwester *my half-sister*	meine Tante *my aunt*
meine Mutter *my mother*	meine Schwester *my sister*	meine Eltern (pl.) *my parents*	mein Opa *my grandpa*
meine Stiefmutter *my stepmother*	meine Stiefschwester *my stepsister*	meine Großeltern (pl.) *my grandparents*	meine Oma *my grandma*

Possessive adjectives

The words *my*, *your*, *his*, *her*, *our* and *their* are called possessive adjectives. In German, the ending of these words changes, depending on whether the noun is masculine, feminine or neuter, and singular or plural. For more details, see **page 141**.

	my	**your**
masculine	mein	dein
feminine	meine	deine
neuter	mein	dein
plural	meine	deine

! Gender of nouns and definite articles ('the')

The German for *the* (= the definite article) depends on the gender of the noun and whether it is singular or plural. The golden rule when memorising vocabulary is always to learn the gender with the noun, so that you can get the correct forms of words to use with it.

der Geburtstag (m.) *birthday*

die Familie (f.) *family*

das Jahre *year*

masculine	der	Der Mann ist lustig.	*The man is funny.*
feminine	die	Die Frau ist lieb.	*The woman is kind.*
neuter	das	Das Meerschweinchen ist froh.	*The guinea pig is happy.*
plural	die	Die Eltern sind toll.	*The parents are great.*

You will see other forms of the definite article later in this book, as it also changes according to the context where it's used. For more details, see **page 137**.

Personality adjectives

Below are examples of interesting adjectives which you can use to describe yourself and others.

ehrlich	*honest*	**lieb**	*loyal, sweet, kind*
freundlich	*friendly*	**nett**	*supportive, nice*
geduldig	*patient*	**offen**	*open, honest*
glücklich	*happy*	**optimistisch**	*optimistic*
hilfsbereit	*helpful*	**toll**	*awesome*
höflich	*polite*	**wunderbar**	*wonderful*

+ Add intensifiers / qualifiers to quantify an adjective:

sehr *very*
ziemlich *quite*
ein bisschen *a bit*

1. Read the following about a family in Germany.

Mein Name ist Viktoria und ich habe eine Patchworkfamilie.
Meine Mutter und ich wohnen zusammen.
In meiner Familie gibt es auch meinen Stiefvater. Er hat zwei Kinder.
Das heißt, ich habe einen Stiefbruder und eine Stiefschwester. Sie sind sehr lieb.
Meine Mutter ist **schwanger**. In ein paar Monaten bekomme ich eine Halbschwester!
Meine Familie ist ein bisschen geduldig und auch ziemlich wunderbar.

Select the correct option to complete each sentence.

1.1 Viktoria ...
A is an only child. **B** has two brothers. **C** has a brother and a sister.

1.2 Her stepfather has ...
A two children. **B** three children. **C** four children.

1.3 In a few months, Viktoria is ...
A leaving home. **B** getting a half-brother. **C** getting a half-sister.

1.4 Viktoria's family is ...
A patient. **B** wonderful. **C** patient and wonderful.

1.1 A 1.2 A 1.3 C 1.4 C

In the reading exam, you will need to interpret unknown words. What does the word **schwanger** in the text above mean? Use the context, i.e. look at the sentence that comes after it, and look at the correct response for 1.3: they will help you work out what it means.

+ The best way to learn vocabulary is to use it! Take this sentence starter: **Mein Bruder ist ...** or if you prefer, start with: **Meine Schwester / Mein Vater / Meine Mutter ist ...**
Choose adjectives and intensifiers and create 10 sentences about this member of your family. Then do another! See intensifiers on **page 144**.

PHYSICAL APPEARANCE

Dein Aussehen — *Physical appearance*

Here are three questions about physical descriptions that someone might ask.

Wie siehst du aus?	Beschreibe eine Person in deiner Familie.
What do you look like?	*Describe a person in your family.*

Wie sieht dein bester Freund oder deine beste Freundin aus?
What does your best friend look like?

ich habe ...	*I have ...*		
er / sie hat ...	*he / she has ...*		
schwarze	*black*	**braune**	*brown*
rote	*red*	**haselnussbraune**	*hazel*
blonde	*blond, fair*	**blaue**	*blue*
kurze	*short*	**grüne**	*green*
lange	*long*	**graue**	*grey*
... Haare	*... hair*	**... Augen**	*... eyes*
einen Rollstuhl	*a wheelchair*	**einen Stock**	*a cane*

ich bin ...	*I am...*
er / sie ist ...	*he / she is ...*
sehr / ziemlich	*very / quite*
groß	*tall*
klein	*short*
dick	*fat*
dünn	*thin*
mittelgroß	*medium height*
behindert / nicht behindert	*disabled / not disabled*

! The adjectives above for hair and eyes are given in their plural form, as written before the noun.

Ich habe blonde Haare und graue Augen. *I have blond hair and blue eyes.*

When you use them after a noun and verb, they do not need the plural **-e** ending. So, to keep it simple, you can use a different phrase and remove the ending, like this:

Meine Haare sind blond und meine Augen sind grau. *My hair is blond and my eyes are grey.*

For more on adjective endings, see **page 140**.

1. You read an online forum where young people describe the person they most admire. Read the four descriptions and find the matching photo for each one.

A

B

C

D

1.1 Ich bewundere meine Großmutter! Sie hat graue Haare und ist ganz lieb.

1.2 Meine Lieblingsperson ist mein Vater. Er sieht gut aus – groß und sportlich.

1.3 Meine Schwester ist supercool. Sie hat rote Haare. Ich finde sie toll.

1.4 Mein Bruder ist fantastisch. Er benutzt einen Rollstuhl und ist sehr geduldig. Er hat braune Haare.

1.1 B   1.2 D   1.3 C   1.4 A

2. Think about three people you admire. Make notes about them, for example, their name, age and birthday, where they live, personality, physical appearance, whether they are family or a friend. Use the example below.

TRACK 4

er/sie heißt	Thorsten
er/sie ist	26
Geburtstag	5. August
wohnt in	München

er/sie ist	cool, ziemlich freundlich
er/sie hat	lange braune Haare, grüne Augen
Familie/Freund/Freundin?	Bruder

Then put your notes into full sentences. Use Exercise 1 to help you.

Read your sentences aloud. Listen to the model answer.

Whatever you can write in German, you should be able to say. Try and reuse language across your writing and speaking, to help you become more confident.

RELATIONSHIPS WITH FAMILY

Wie verstehst du dich mit ...? *How do you get on with ...?*

It is important to add detail. Relationships with the people around you are not just good or bad! One way to do this is to describe the relationship generally (F and H), and then add a reason to back that up, mentioning positive and negative aspects (H).

Generally ...	
im Allgemeinen	*in general*
im Großen und Ganzen	*generally speaking*
generell	*in general*

More specifically ...	
manchmal	*sometimes*
einerseits anderseits	*on the one hand on the other hand*
jedoch	*however*

1. You read about two people's relationship with someone in their family. Answer the questions, giving the correct name each time, Simone or Leopold.

Ich verstehe mich im Allgemeinen gut mit meinem Bruder. Er ist einerseits sehr lieb und freundlich. Er ist aber auch manchmal nervig und wir streiten uns. **Simone**

Meine Großmutter ist generell fantastisch. Sie kann mich manchmal nicht verstehen, aber sie hilft mir mit meinen Problemen. **Leopold**

1.1 Who gets on generally with their relative?
1.2 Whose relative is fantastic?
1.3 Who describes their relative as friendly?
1.4 Whose relative can sometimes be annoying?
1.5 Whose relative helps them when they have problems?
1.6 Who argues with their relative?

1.1 Simone 1.2 Leopold 1.3 Simone 1.4 Simone 1.5 Leopold 1.6 Simone

2. You listen to a radio phone-in show. Three people talk about their relationships with family and friends. Select the most relevant statement for each person. (2.1–2.3)

TRACK 5

A	My partner is very supportive of me.	D	My father is always positive.
B	My parents are quite negative about my future.	E	My sister and I do not always get along well.
C	My partner makes fun of me.	F	My father and I talk about everything.

2.1 F 2.2 E 2.3 A

Reflexive pronouns and verbs

Reflexive pronouns refer back to a person or a thing, e.g. myself, yourself, themselves.

mich	*myself, me*	sich	*himself, herself, itself, themselves*
dich	*yourself*	uns	*ourselves*

When you use a reflexive verb, a reflexive pronoun is always needed, after the verb. See the underlined words in the examples below.

Infinitive		Example	
sich interessieren für	*to be interested in*	Ich interessiere mich für Musik.	*I am interested in music.*
sich kümmern um	*to look after*	Wir kümmern uns um unsere Mutter.	*We look after our mother.*
sich streiten	*to argue*	Ich streite mich mit meinem Bruder.	*I argue with my brother.*
sich verstehen mit	*to get on with*	Er versteht sich gut mit seiner Schwester.	*He gets on well with his sister.*

3. Translate the sentences below into **German**.
   - 3.1 I get on well with my stepbrother.
   - 3.2 My brother is interested in film.
   - 3.3 My sister looks after the dog.
   - 3.4 My parents look after my grandmother.

3.1 Ich verstehe mich gut mit meinem Stiefbruder. 3.2. Mein Bruder interessiert sich für Film. 3.3 Meine Schwester kümmert sich um den Hund. 3.4 Meine Eltern kümmern sich um unsere Großmutter.

FRIENDSHIPS

Ein guter Freund / Eine gute Freundin — *A good friend*

You can describe a friend's personality and then expand in further detail.

mein Freund ist ... meine Freundin ist ...	*my friend is ...*
hilfsbereit	*helpful*
treu	*loyal*
ehrlich	*honest*
höflich	*polite*
lustig	*funny*
ruhig	*calm*

ein guter Freund ... eine gute Freundin ...	*a good friend ...*
hört dir zu	*listens to you*
hält deine Probleme geheim	*keeps your problems a secret*
ist immer für dich da	*is always there for you*
gibt gute Ratschläge	*gives good advice*
lügt nie	*never lies*
teilt seine/ihre Interessen mit dir	*shares your interests*
lacht mit dir	*laughs with you*

Reading aloud

TRACK 6

1. A documentary maker visits your school and interviews students about what makes a good friend. You are asked to talk about your friend. Read the text below out loud. Listen to the recording and check your pronunciation.

Meine Freundin ist sehr nett und ganz ehrlich.

Sie versteht sich gut mit allen.

Ich finde sie prima, denn sie ist immer für mich da.

Wir machen viel zusammen und lachen miteinander.

Ein guter Freund oder eine gute Freundin unterstützt dich.

! Make sure you understand the key messages in what you read. Then make a note of useful phrases so you can adapt and reuse them for your own writing and speaking tasks.

The present tense of regular verbs

Use the present tense to say what you and others do or are doing.

English has two different kinds of present tense: we say, for example, *I listen* to describe something we do generally or regularly, but we use *I am listening* to say what we are doing now. In German, it is just one version of the present tense you need to remember, for both of these.

+ German is generally considered a pattern-based language. What works for one verb in the present tense works for the majority.

Forming the regular present tense

Infinitive: **lachen** *to laugh* – this is the 'core' verb, the version you would find in the dictionary. Now change the ending. By adding the pronoun and the ending, you can use the verb to express your and other people's regular or ongoing actions.

ich	*I*	lache	*I laugh, I am laughing*
du	*you*	lachst	*you laugh, you are laughing*
er / sie / es	*he / she / it*	lacht	*he / she / it laughs, he / she / it is laughing*
wir	*we*	lachen	*we laugh, we are laughing*
ihr	*you (plural)*	lacht	*you laugh, you are laughing*
sie	*they*	lachen	*they laugh, they are laughing*
Sie	*you (formal)*	lachen	*you laugh, you are laughing*

For more information on the present tense, see **page 148**.

2. Your friend watched your interview in the documentary about friendship and sent you a text. Unfortunately, your phone screen is cracked and some letters are not very clear. Fill in the missing verb endings (1–10) to complete the text.

Susi! Das Interview war toll! Du bist so lieb. Ich schätz___ (1) deine Freundschaft. Wenn ich traurig bin, ruf___ (2) ich dich an und wir red___ (3) über Probleme und find___ (4) Lösungen! Du sag___ (5) mir immer, was ich machen soll.

Man mach___ (6) viel für Freunde: er oder sie hör___ (7) mit dir Musik, koch___ (8), geh___ (9) ins Kino!

Wir mach___ (10) viel zusammen. Wie toll! Tschüss, LG, Holly

1. -e 2. -e 3. -en 4. -en 5. -st 6. -t 7. -t 8. -t 9. -t 10. -en

Challenge yourself in your writing exam! Writing accurate sentences in the third person (using **er**, **sie**, **es**) allows you to talk about a wider group of people, not just yourself.

IDENTITY AND RELATIONSHIPS WITH OTHERS

Zusammensetzen *Putting it all together*

1. Categorise the words and phrases below: copy them into the grid of identity subtopics.

meine Kleidung | höflich | meine Eltern | meine Großeltern

Musik | Kino | freundlich | Haar und Haarfarbe

Schreiben | mein bester Freund | optimistisch | Theater

mein Aussehen	**meine Interessen**
meine Familie und Freunde	**meine Persönlichkeit**

mein Aussehen: *meine Kleidung, Haar und Haarfarbe*
meine Interessen: *Theater, Schreiben, Musik, Kino*
meine Familie und Freunde: *meine Eltern, meine Großeltern, mein bester Freund*
meine Persönlichkeit: *optimistisch, freundlich, höflich*

Dictation

TRACK 7

2. Use the words above to help you with this dictation task. You will hear **three** sentences. Listen and write in **German** the sentences you hear.

2.1 Ich liebe meine Großeltern, denn sie sind so freundlich.

2.2 Mein bester Freund hat lange, lockige und blaue Haare.

2.3 Meine Familie interessiert sich für Musik und Kino.

You will hear each sentence three times. Use the first time to listen for key words, the second time to transcribe the sentence in full, and the third time to check for accuracy, i.e. spelling, verb endings, adjectival endings.

Zusammensetzen continued

3. Translate the following sentences into **German**.
   - 3.1 My name is Hannah and I am fourteen years old.
   - 3.2 I have long blond hair and green eyes.
   - 3.3 My brother is from Germany and lives in Vienna.
   - 3.4 I get on well with my brother.
   - 3.5 My family is very friendly but sometimes annoying.

3.1 Ich heiße Hannah und ich bin vierzehn Jahre alt.

3.2 Ich habe lange blonde Haare und grüne Augen.

3.3 Mein Bruder kommt aus Deutschland und wohnt in Wien.

3.4 Ich verstehe mich gut mit meinem Bruder.

3.5 Meine Familie ist sehr freundlich, aber manchmal ärgerlich.

\+ Now write out the sentences and change the details to make them correct for you.

To help you, look back through the pages of this topic to find words you want to use.

Role play

TRACK 8

4. You are talking to a German friend. Use what you have learned to prepare answers to these questions. Play the recording and pause after each question to give yourself time to answer. When you see this **–?–** you will have to ask a question.
   - 4.1 Say what you think a good friend should be. (Give **one** detail.)
   - 4.2 Say what your friend is like. (Give **two** details.)
   - 4.3 Describe your relationship with someone in your family. (Give **one** detail.)
   - 4.4 Say whether you want to get married. (Give **one** detail.)
   - **?** 4.5 Ask your German friend what they are like.

   Compare your responses with the sample answers below. See if you can come up with another set of answers.

Example answer: 4.1 Ein guter Freund/Eine gute Freundin lacht mit dir. 4.2 Mein Freund/Meine Freundin ist ruhig und hilfsbereit. 4.3 Ich verstehe mich gut mit meiner Mutter. 4.4 Ich will nicht heiraten. 4.5 Wie bist du als Person?

FOOD AND DRINK

Was du isst und trinkst — *What you eat and drink*

Here is a list of food and drink items.

der Tee	*tea*	das Obst	*fruit*	das Brot	*bread*
der Kaffee	*coffee*	der Kuchen	*cake*	die Marmelade	*jam*
das Wasser	*water*	das Eis	*ice cream*	der Fisch	*fish*
die Pommes (pl.)	*chips*	die Milch	*milk*	der Alkohol	*alcohol*
der Käse	*cheese*	das Gemüse	*vegetables*	der Wein	*wine*
die Cola	*cola*	die Wurst	*sausage*	das Fleisch	*meat*
der Zucker	*sugar*	der Saft	*juice*	das Hähnchen	*chicken*

1. You hear a radio item about a local survey of young people's diet choices. Listen and then complete the following sentences about it with the missing words in **English**.

TRACK 9

1.1 65% of the participants are vegetarian and do not eat any __________ or meat.

1.2 70% like to drink __________ or tea with __________ and __________ .

1.3 Around 75% sometimes eat __________ , so __________ or fries.

1.4 Fewer than 25% of them drink __________ , either __________ or __________ .

1.5 Almost everyone drinks at least two litres of __________ a day.

1.1 fish 1.2 coffee, milk, sugar 1.3 fast food, pizza 1.4 alcohol, wine, beer 1.5 water

Read the sentences first, before playing the recording. From the context, can you make logical guesses for the missing words?

Write notes on the listening exercise the first time you listen. You can note the words you hear in German first, if you wish, or translate them into English for the sentences. When you listen a second time, use the notes to help you understand the text in greater detail.

German and English come from the same language family. Although the pronunciation often differs, cognates across the two languages are very common. See how many you can deduce.

Was du isst und trinkst continued

2. What do you eat? Fill in the meal plan: write at least **three** food items and **one** drink for each meal, in **German**.

	zum Frühstück ***for breakfast***	**zum Mittagessen** ***for lunch***	**zum Abendessen** ***for dinner***
ich esse	*Brot mit Butter und Marmelade*		
ich trinke	*Tee*		

Then, using that plan, write a sentence about each meal, for example:

Ich esse zum Frühstück Brot mit Butter und Marmelade und ich trinke Tee.
Ich esse zum Mittagessen ...

Word order: the verb as second idea

The verb is a powerful part of speech. There are rules about word order and where we can expect to hear or see the verb in any German sentence. In German, the verb is the second idea, but this does not mean the second word: think of it as the second new item of information in a German sentence.

1st item – subject	2nd item – verb	3rd item	4th item
Ich	esse	zum Abendessen	Wurst.
Mein Bruder	hat	oft	Hunger.
Wir	trinken	am liebsten	heiße Getränke.
Meine Schwester	kocht	am Wochenende	Essen.

You can start your sentence with details about when or how, and then you invert (swap) the verb and its subject, so that you keep the verb as the second idea in that part of the sentence.

1st item	2nd item – verb	3rd item – subject	4th item
Zum Abendessen	esse	ich	Wurst.
Oft	hat	mein Bruder	Hunger.
Am liebsten	trinken	wir	heiße Getränke.
Am Wochenende	kocht	meine Schwester	Essen.

Revise your sentences about meals, to make them start with the meal phrase:
Zum Frühstück esse ich Brot mit Butter und Marmelade und ich trinke Tee.

Applying variety to your language in this way will give you extra credit. Practise different word order often, to become more fluent in using these rules and increase your marks in the exam.

For more rules on word order and word order with verbs, see **page 154**.

EATING HEALTHILY

Gesund bleiben — *Staying healthy*

You can use these verbs to express your opinion.

ich liebe	ich mag	ich mag ... nicht	ich hasse
I love	*I like*	*I do not like*	*I hate*

You can also express what you like or do not like to eat and drink by using **gern**, **nicht gern** and **am liebsten**.

Ich esse gern Hähnchen mit Kartoffeln und Salat. *I like to eat chicken with potatoes and salad.*
Ich trinke nicht gern Cola oder Orangensaft. *I don't like drinking coke or orange juice.*
Meine Familie und ich essen am liebsten Nudeln. *My family and I like eating pasta most of all.*

Whether it's a special occasion, a meal out with family, or a takeaway with friends, here are some useful words when ordering a meal out.

eine Flasche	ein Glas	die Speisekarte	das Gericht
bottle	*glass*	*menu*	*dish, plate of food*

1. Four friends are at a restaurant for Jakob's birthday and discuss what they will order. Read each text aloud, then listen to the recording to check your pronunciation.

TRACK 10

Heute ist mein Geburtstag! Ich bestelle Hähnchen mit Pommes und ich möchte ein Glas Limonade trinken. Dann essen wir Schokoladenkuchen. **Jakob**

Ich möchte gesund essen, aber ich liebe Schokoladenkuchen. Also bestelle ich Tomatensuppe mit Salat und kein Brot. Nur Wasser für mich. **Lina**

Normalerweise koche ich nur gesundes Essen. Heute bestelle ich Schnitzel mit Kartoffelsalat. Ich trinke ein Glas Wein. **Pelin**

Ich bin Veganer, also bestelle ich das Gericht mit Gemüse und Tofu. Das schmeckt gut! Ein Glas Cola für mich. **Thorsten**

! Refer to the phonics page to help guide your pronunciation. The **st** in **bestelle** is like a *sht* sound. Try to read the texts aloud with some intonation, as though you were talking to friends. Take the time to practise them multiple times, to improve your fluency and level of confidence.

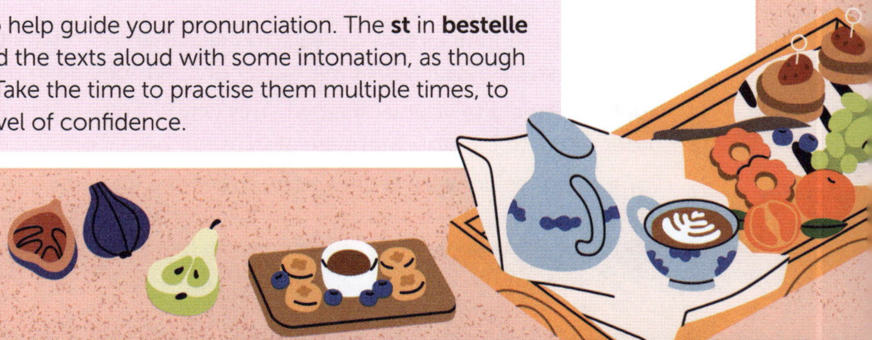

The *um ... zu ...* construction

To give a reason for doing something, you can use **um ... zu ...**, which means *to* or *in order to ...*

On **page 21** verbs had to be the second idea. Here, the 'core' form of the verb, the infinitive, is always at the end, after the other details. Compare the German and English word order in these examples.

	fit		**bleiben**	*to stay fit*
	gesund		**essen**	*to eat healthily*
um	**jeden Tag leckeres Essen**	**zu**	**kochen**	*to cook tasty food every day*
	in Form		**sein**	*to be fit*
	immer meine Familie		**unterstützen**	*to always support my family*
	oft mit meinem Bruder		**sprechen**	*to speak often with my brother*

+ It's valuable to be able to transfer your knowledge and use a construction that you've learned across different contexts. The examples above relate to the topics in sections 1.1 and 1.2, but you'll be able to apply the same patterns in your speaking and writing across all the other topics.

2. Translate these sentences into **German**.
   2.1 I like to cook every day.
   2.2 What do you eat at the weekend?
   2.3 My brother likes to order German dishes.
   2.4 I eat vegetables every day, in order to be in shape.
   2.5 We never drink alcohol, in order to stay healthy.

   2.1 Ich koche gern jeden Tag. / Ich koche jeden Tag gern. / Ich mag jeden Tag kochen.
   2.2 Was isst du am Wochenende?
   2.3 Mein Bruder bestellt gern deutsche Gerichte.
   2.4 Ich esse jeden Tag Gemüse, / Jeden Tag esse ich Gemüse, um in Form zu sein.
   2.5 Wir trinken nie Alkohol, um gesund zu bleiben.

There may be more than one way of translating the sentences successfully.

Think about how you apply your knowledge of verb endings and word order. For example, sentence 2.1 could also be **Jeden Tag koche ich gern**.

BEING ACTIVE

Sport und Fitness — *Sport and exercise*

ich mache ...	*I do ...*
Reiten	*horse riding*
Leichtathletik	*athletics*
Yoga	*yoga*

ich spiele ...	*I play ...*
Fußball	*football*
Basketball	*basketball*
Rugby	*rugby*
Badminton	*badminton*
Tennis	*tennis*

ich fahre Rad	*I cycle*
ich gehe schwimmen	*I go swimming*
ich gehe spazieren	*I go for a walk*
ich gehe ins Fitnesszentrum	*I go to the gym*
in die Turnhalle	*to the sports hall*
draußen	*outside*

1. You are in a PE lesson with your Austrian penpal at their school in Linz. Listen to the PE teacher talk through the different sports and activities on offer. Select the correct sport for Group A, Group B and Group C.

TRACK 11

1	Weights and training
2	Swimming
3	Tennis
4	Basketball
5	Football

Group A: 3   *Group B: 2*   *Group C: 5*

!

Recognising individual words is an important step to learning the vocabulary. However, learning its meaning in context is vital to developing confidence with producing the vocabulary in your own written and spoken work.

Make time to listen to this and other listening exercises multiple times; find the transcript online and follow it to help you understand what you are hearing.

Word order: time, manner, place

You'll often want to add details to your sentences. In German, they are organised into a specific order: **time** (when you do an activity), **manner** (how you do it, or with whom), **place** (where).

Type of detail	Linked question word	Examples
Time	Wann? *When?*	jeden Tag, normalerweise, ab und zu, oft, am Wochenende, montags, viermal pro Woche, morgens, abends, manchmal
Manner	Wie? *How?*	mit Freunden, mit meiner Familie, mit meinem Bruder, allein, mit meiner Klasse, mit meinen Eltern, mit meinem Handy
Place	Wo? *Where?*	in der Schule, zu Hause, im Fitnessstudio, in der Turnhalle, im Restaurant, im Imbiss, in einem Café, im Park

Ich treibe jeden Tag allein im Fitnessstudio Sport, um gesund zu bleiben.
I play sport every day on my own in the gym, in order to stay healthy.

Meine Mutter trinkt oft mit Freunden in einem Café Tee.
My mother often drinks tea with friends in a cafe.

2. Three people have contributed to a forum online about their health and fitness regime. Read the posts and answer the questions below in **English**.

Ich jogge viermal pro Woche allein im Park, um in Form zu bleiben. Ich bin nicht so schnell wie meine Freunde. **Jens**

In der Schule spiele ich mit meiner Klasse Basketball, und freitags mache ich mit meinem Trainer im Fitnessstudio Training. Ich bin sehr stark und aktiv. **Sara**

Mein Freund und ich sind nicht sehr sportlich, aber wir gehen am Wochenende in die Disko, um zu tanzen. Wir bewegen uns und haben Spaß! **Layla**

2.1 Who does sport on their own?
2.2 Who does not like doing sport?
2.3 Who says their regime makes them strong?
2.4 Who has someone helping them get fit?
2.5 Who does a fitness activity outside?
2.6 Who is more active at the weekend?

2.1 Jens 2.2 Layla 2.3 Sara 2.4 Sara 2.5 Jens 2.6 Layla

Before looking at the questions, read the texts. Highlight the words you recognise and make notes around the text about what you understand. This will help you to identify the answers more confidently.

Can you spot examples of the 'time, manner, place' rule in the forum posts above? When you attempt a writing task on this topic, refer back here for model sentences.

ACHES AND PAINS

Mein Körper *My body*

mein Bauch *my stomach*	mein Finger *my finger*	mein Fuß *my foot*	mein Kopf *my head*	mein Mund *my mouth*	mein Rücken *my back*
meine Hand *my hand*	meine Nase *my nose*	mein Auge *my eye*	mein Bein *my leg*	mein Herz *my heart*	mein Zahn *my tooth*
		mein Körper *my body*	mein Ohr *my ear*		

To say how long something has been hurting, use **seit** (*since, for + a length of time*).

Note that the verb **tut** is in the present tense – don't try to translate 'has been hurting' into a past tense.

Mein Finger tut seit drei Tagen weh. *My finger has been hurting for three days.*
Mein Auge tut seit einer Woche weh. *My eye has been hurting for a week.*
Mein Herz tut seit einem Monat weh. *My heart has been hurting for a month.*

Dictation

TRACK 12

1. Listen to the five sentences. Write them out in **German**.

1.1 Mein Bauch tut seit zwei Tagen weh.
1.2 Mein Kopf tut seit einer Woche weh.
1.3 Mein Auge tut seit drei Wochen weh.
1.4 Ich habe seit einem Monat Kopfschmerzen.
1.5 Ich spiele normalerweise Fußball, aber mein Fuß tut weh.

+ 1.5 links two short phrases with a conjunction: **aber** (*but*). When you write or speak, use a conjunction to bring in additional or contrasting detail, and to add variety.

In the dictation task, you will hear each sentence repeated three times: the first time as a full sentence, the second time in short sections, and the third time again as a full sentence.

You will be expected to use your phonetic knowledge to spell out two unknown German words, like **Kopfschmerzen** in sentence 1.4 above. Always attempt to spell every word – don't leave any gaps. You may still be awarded marks for the effort, even if accuracy is uneven.

The perfect tense with *haben*

The perfect tense is used for events that happened in the past and recent actions that are now completed. It consists of the present tense of **haben** (or **sein**, see **page 28**) and the past participle of the main verb.

Auxiliary verb phrase	Detail	Past participle
	Essen	**gekocht** *cooked*
ich habe	Fußball	**gespielt** *played*
meine Schwester hat	nicht genug	**geschlafen** *slept*
wir haben	Kaffee	**getrunken** *drunk*
	etwas	**gegessen** *eaten*

For more on the perfect tense with **haben** and with **sein**, and how to form past participles, see **pages 149-150**.

!

Remember to put the past participle at the end of the sentence or the phrase.

There can be more than one detail in the middle, keeping the time, manner, place sequence. When we translate into English, the words may need to appear in a different order to make the English sentence sound fluent.

Ich habe gestern allein zu Hause Essen gekocht.
I cooked food at home yesterday on my own.

2. Circle the perfect tense verb in each sentence. Remember, there are two parts to it. Then translate the sentences into **English**.

2.1 Ich habe mir mit einem Fußball im Park meinen Fuß verletzt.

2.2 Ich habe im Restaurant Hamburger mit Pommes gegessen und jetzt tut mein Bauch weh.

2.3 Mein Bruder hat nicht genug geschlafen und er ist sehr müde.

2.1 habe ... verletzt – I injured my foot with a football in the park.

2.2 habe ... gegessen – I ate a hamburger with chips at the restaurant and now my stomach hurts.

2.3 hat ... geschlafen – My brother did not sleep enough / hasn't slept enough and he is very tired.

PREVIOUS AND CURRENT LIFESTYLE

Damals und jetzt — *Back then and now*

Here are some phrases to write about health and lifestyle habits in the past. The verbs are in the perfect tense.

	Auxiliary verb phrase	Detail	Past participle
with **haben**	ich **habe**	Gemüse	**gegessen** *eaten*
	mein Halbbruder **hat**	Wasser	**getrunken** *drank*
	meine Schwester **hat**	Sport	**gemacht** *did*
	wir **haben**	Videospiele	**gespielt** *played*
with **sein**	ich **bin** mein Vater **ist** meine Mutter **ist** wir **sind**	laufen joggen schwimmen	**gegangen** *went*

!

Perfect tense: haben or sein?

Verbs that involve movement or state use **sein** to make the perfect tense, e.g. **ich bin gegangen** (*I went*), **sie ist geblieben** (*she stayed*).

Other verbs use **haben**, e.g. **wir haben gespielt** (*we played*). For more about this, see **page 149**.

1. Reorder the words to make sentences that match the English translations. You'll need to give the first word a capital letter and add a full stop at the end of the sentence.

   1.1 ich / in den Park / gegangen / bin / gestern / ich / habe / gespielt / Fußball / mit Freunden / und
   I went to the park yesterday and I played football with friends.

   1.2 ich / Pizza / gegessen / habe / am Imbiss / vor zwei Tagen / mit meiner Familie
   Two days ago I ate pizza with my family at the snack stand.

   1.3 mein Bruder / geschwommen / ist / letzte Woche / um / bleiben / zu / gesund
   My brother swam last week, in order to stay healthy.

   1.4 mein Vater / gestern Abend / hat / gekocht / für uns / leckeres / Essen
   My father cooked delicious food for us yesterday.

1.1 Ich bin gestern in den Park gegangen und ich habe mit Freunden Fußball gespielt.
1.2 Ich habe vor zwei Tagen mit meiner Familie am Imbiss Pizza gegessen.
1.3 Mein Bruder ist letzte Woche geschwommen, um gesund zu bleiben.
1.4 Mein Vater hat gestern Abend für uns leckeres Essen gekocht.

!

Don't forget to practise variety in your word order. You can rewrite those sentences, starting with the time phrase, then inverting the verb, e.g. **Gestern bin ich in den Park gegangen und habe Fußball mit Freunden gespielt. Letzte Woche ist mein Bruder geschwommen, um ...**

Damals und jetzt continued

Use sequencers to link a fact about your previous lifestyle with one about your current lifestyle.

Sequencer for past events	
als Kind	*as a child*
damals	*back then*
früher	*previously, in former times*

Sequencer for current events	
heute	*today, now*
heutzutage	*nowadays*
jetzt	*now*

Ich habe als Kind nur Milch getrunken. Jetzt trinke ich zwei Liter Wasser pro Tag.
As a child I only drank milk. Now I drink two litres of water a day.

Ich habe damals keinen Sport gemacht. Heute mache ich fünfmal pro Woche Sport.
I did not do any sport back then. Now I do sport five times a week.

2. You read about a German influencer's previous and current lifestyles. Read the text and answer the questions below in **English**.

Ich bin 25 Jahre alt und bin Influencer für Mode und Musik. Die Gesundheit ist mir wirklich sehr wichtig. Jedoch war ich als Kind gar nicht gesund! Ich war sehr faul und habe nichts für meine Fitness gemacht. Ich hatte keine Zeit! Heute bleibe ich aktiv und ich gehe fast jeden Tag joggen oder schwimmen. Ich fühle mich nicht müde.

Auch habe ich oft Süßigkeiten gegessen, fast jeden Tag! Das war zu viel. Jetzt koche ich mit meiner Familie zu Hause. Ich liebe es, im Restaurant frische Salate oder Fisch zu bestellen, um Protein zu essen und stark zu bleiben.

Als Jugendlicher habe ich Zigaretten geraucht. Natürlich ist das gar nicht gesund, und für die Lungen sehr gefährlich. Heutzutage rauche ich nicht.

Manchmal trinke ich ein Glas Wein oder Bier, aber ich brauche es nicht.

2.1 What was this person's health like as a child? Give **two** details.
2.2 What do they do regularly in the week now? Give **one** detail.
2.3 How does regular fitness make them feel?
2.4 What did they eat too much of as a child?
2.5 Why do they order salad or fish when they go out? Give **one** reason.
2.6 Why did they stop smoking? Give **one** detail.

2.1 (any two of:) not healthy, very lazy, did not do anything for their fitness; 2.2 (one of:) jogging, swimming; 2.3 not tired; 2.4 sweets; 2.5 (one of:) to get protein, to stay strong; 2.6 (one of:) it's not at all healthy, dangerous for the lungs

!

The imperfect tense

There is another kind of past tense, the imperfect tense. The most useful ones are the imperfect of **haben** – **ich hatte** (*I had*) – and the imperfect of **sein** – **ich war** (*I was*), **das war** (*that was*). Spot **ich war** and **ich hatte** in the text above. For more details on the imperfect tense, see **page 151**.

HEALTHY LIVING AND LIFESTYLE

Zusammensetzen *Putting it all together*

1. You hear some callers to a radio programme talk about diet and lifestyle, in their childhood and nowadays. Fill in the table with the details in **English**.

TRACK 13

		Habits in the past	Current habits
1.1	Franziska		
1.2	Henrik		
1.3	Lars		

1.1 Past: did not eat bananas, Present: eats at least five pieces of fruit a day

1.2 Past: went skiing (with family, in the winter), Present: goes to fitness centre/gym (very often)

1.3 Past: did sport every day at school (table tennis or basketball), Present: plays football in the garden (with brother).

Role play

TRACK 14

2. You are talking to a German friend. Use what you have learned to prepare answers to these questions. Play the recording and pause after each question to give yourself time to answer. When you see this **–?–** you will have to ask a question.
   - 2.1 Say what exercise you do. (Give **one** detail.)
   - 2.2 Say how often you do sport. (Give **one** detail.)
   - 2.3 Describe your current lifestyle. (Give **two** details.)
   - 2.4 Give your opinion on fast food and explain why.
   - **?** 2.5 Ask your friend a question about their lifestyle.

Model response: 2.1 Ich mache Leichtathletik. 2.2 Ich mache jeden Tag Sport. 2.3 Ich spiele normalerweise Fußball und ich esse Fastfood. 2.4 Ich liebe Fastfood. Es ist billig und lecker. 2.5 Was machst du, um gesund zu bleiben?

Zusammensetzen continued

3. This student has written **25 words** about their exercise and diet routine, in answer to the first bullet point of this task. The full task would require **90 words**, for all three bullet points. Mention:
   - your exercise and diet routine
   - what you have recently done for your routine
   - what you will do tomorrow for your health.

> Zu Hause koche ich immer und esse normalerweise Fleisch mit Salat. Meine Mutter spielt jeden Tag mit ihrem Trainer im Fitnesszentrum Tennis. Manchmal schwimmen wir draußen.

Use the ideas in the table below to suggest **six** other possible sentences for the first bullet point.

Verb (infinitive)	Time	Manner	Place
essen	heute	allein	draußen
trinken	immer	mit dem Fahrrad	im Fitnesszentrum
laufen	jetzt	mit meiner Familie	zu Hause
joggen	manchmal	mit Freunden	im Park
schwimmen	normalerweise	zu Fuß	im Restaurant
kochen	jeden Tag	mit dem Trainer	in der Schule
spielen	fünfmal pro Woche	mit der Trainerin	
schlafen	acht Stunden		

+ You can refer to the transcripts of Exercise 1 and your answers for Exercise 2 to help you formulate the sentences and add any extra detail.

★ **Add variety to your sentences by varying the word order and bringing in vocabulary from other topics. This will help you to reach the top bands on the mark scheme.**

4. Now it's your turn! You have been asked to write a post for a healthy lifestyle blog. Use the ideas from Exercises 1, 2 and 3, in addition to your other knowledge. Write approximately **90 words** in **German**. Describe:
   - your exercise and diet routine
   - what you have recently done for your routine
   - what you will do tomorrow for your health.

4. Model answer: Ich bin in Form. Normalerweise esse ich zu Hause Eier und ich trinke Orangensaft. Das ist sehr gut für die Gesundheit. Sport ist nicht so wichtig für mich, aber ich bin relativ aktiv. Gestern bin ich mit Freunden im Park joggen gegangen, um mich gut und stark zu fühlen. Aber mein Bruder ist zu Hause geblieben und hat nur auf dem Sofa Popcorn gegessen. Er macht nicht genug Sport. Morgen gehe ich joggen und dann mache ich Yoga.

SCHOOL AND SCHOOL SUBJECTS

Was lernst du gern? *What do you like learning?*

Check you know your school subjects in German.

Ich lerne gern / Mein Lieblingsfach ist		*I like learning / My favourite subject is*	
Englisch	*English*	**Biologie**	*biology*
Deutsch	*German*	**Physik**	*physics*
Spanisch	*Spanish*	**Chemie**	*chemistry*
Französisch	*French*	**Naturwissenschaften**	*science*
Geschichte	*history*	**Mathe**	*maths*
Kunst	*art*	**Religion**	*religious studies / RE*
Kochen	*cookery / food tech*	**Musik**	*music*
Informatik	*ICT*	**Sport**	*PE*
Erdkunde	*geography*	**Theater**	*drama*

! Take care with the pronunciation of cognates. When you hear German words like **Biologie** and **Sport**, listen carefully and repeat the pronunciation, to be sure you don't say them like English words.

1. Read these comments from students on social media. Which subject does each student like best and least, and why?

Ich bin nicht sehr kreativ, also lerne ich gar nicht gern Kunst. Mein Lieblingsfach ist Informatik, denn ich finde Computer faszinierend. Sie sind für die Arbeit und die moderne Welt wirklich nützlich. **Pelin**

Ich hasse Theater. Ich bin einfach nicht talentiert. Sport ist besser, aber ich lerne am liebsten Kochen. Ich möchte in einem Restaurant arbeiten. **Stefan**

Ich lerne nicht gern Sprachen. Ich finde Englisch schwer und ich verstehe sehr wenig. Naturwissenschaften sind viel besser, denn sie sind logisch und wichtig. **Sophia**

Erkunde ist toll, aber Englisch ist mein Lieblingsfach. Ich möchte an der Universität Literatur studieren, denn ich will in einer Schule als Lehrer arbeiten. Ich lerne nicht gern Religion. Es ist für mich nicht interessant. **Manuel**

Pelin: *likes ICT best (finds computers fascinating, useful for work and modern world). Dislikes art (is not very creative).* ***Stefan:*** *likes food tech (would like to work in a restaurant). Dislikes drama (isn't talented).* ***Sophia:*** *likes science (it's logical and important). Dislikes languages (finds English hard and does not understand much).* ***Manuel:*** *likes geography, but English is his favourite subject (wants to study literature and work as a teacher in a school). Dislikes religious studies (not interesting to him).*

Was lernst du gern? continued

2. Talk about the subjects you like and dislike, and give reasons why, using the grid below.

<table>
<tr><td>Ich lerne</td><td>gern
lieber
am liebsten</td><td rowspan="4">(school subject),</td><td rowspan="4">denn</td><td>es ist / sie sind
die Gruppenarbeit ist
die Klassenarbeit ist
die Stunden sind</td><td colspan="2">einfach / leicht.
interessant / kreativ.
nützlich / praktisch.
schwer / schwierig.</td></tr>
<tr><td>Ich lerne</td><td>nicht gern
gar nicht gern</td><td colspan="3">es gibt keine / viele Hausaufgaben.</td></tr>
<tr><td colspan="2" rowspan="2">Ich hasse</td><td rowspan="2">der Lehrer
die Lehrerin</td><td>ist</td><td>gemein.
hilfsbereit.
höflich.
streng.</td></tr>
<tr><td colspan="2">hilft uns (nicht).</td></tr>
</table>

! Be careful when you use the word **lieber** (column 2). It is easily confused with **ich liebe** (*I love*). You need to use **lieber** straight after a verb, e.g. **Ich lerne lieber Deutsch** (*I prefer learning German*) or **Ich spiele lieber mit Freunden** (*I prefer playing with friends*).

3. Listen to four students (3.1–3.4) giving reasons for liking their favourite subjects. What subject do they pick and what reason do they give? Note the subject in **English** and write the correct letter for the reason.

TRACK 15

A	group work	D	helpful teacher
B	no homework	E	useful for future work
C	the subject is practical	F	loves travelling

3.1 maths, C 3.2 geography, F 3.3 music, B 3.4 English, D

SCHOOL FACILITIES AND UNIFORM

Was gibt es in deiner Schule? *What is your school like?*

1. Read this description of Lilian's school. Find the German for the words and phrases below.

Meine Schule ist im Stadtzentrum. Die Gegend ist nicht sehr sauber, aber das Schulgebäude ist ziemlich neu und modern. Drinnen gibt es eine praktische Turnhalle für die Sportstunden und für die Tanzstunden nach der Schule. Draußen haben wir einen schönen Sportplatz für die Fußball- und Rugbyspiele.

Außerdem haben wir eine fantastische Bibliothek. Sie hat viele interessante Bücher und auch Schreibtische und Computer, um für Klassenarbeiten zu lernen. Es gibt viele bequeme Klassenzimmer für die Schüler und Lehrer und drei Chemielabore.

In der Pause gibt es eine enorme Kantine – man kann dort etwas zu essen oder trinken kaufen. Draußen gibt es auch einen großen Schulhof. Da können wir in den Pausen mit Freunden reden, denn wir haben nicht jede Stunde zusammen. **Lilian**

1.1 school building	1.5 library	1.9 students
1.2 sports hall	1.6 desks	1.10 (science) labs
1.3 PE lessons	1.7 school tests	1.11 in the break time
1.4 playing field	1.8 classrooms	1.12 school yard

2. Read the text again and complete the following sentences. Select the correct option.
   - 2.1 Lilian's school is **new and modern / not very clean / old.**
   - 2.2 The indoor gym is used for PE lessons and **detentions after school / clubs / dance classes.**
   - 2.3 Students come to the library because it **is comfortable / has lots of interesting books / is a good a place to chat to friends.**
   - 2.4 To get something to eat or drink, students can **buy something from a shop nearby / bring something from home / use the canteen.**
   - 2.5 In the school yard, students chat to **friends from different classes / friends / teachers.**

1. 1.1 Schulgebäude 1.2 Turnhalle 1.3 Sportstunden 1.4 Sportplatz 1.5 Bibliothek 1.6 Schreibtische 1.7 Klassenarbeit 1.8 Klassenzimmer 1.9 Schüler 1.10 Chemielabore 1.11 in der Pause 1.12 Schulhof

2. 2.1 new and modern 2.2 dance classes 2.3 has lots of interesting books 2.4 use the canteen 2.5 friends from different classes

! Be careful not to get confused between **Schule** (*school*) and **Schüler** (*school student*(s)).

3. Using Lilian's description as a model, write a paragraph to describe your own school.

Wie ist deine Schuluniform? *What is your unifom like?*

Here is some useful vocabulary for school uniform.

die Hose	*(a pair of) trousers*
der Rock	*skirt*
das Hemd	*shirt*
die Jacke	*jacket*
die Krawatte	*tie*
die Socken (pl.)	*socks*
die Schuhe (pl.)	*shoes*

schwarz	*black*
weiß	*white*
grün	*green*
gelb	*yellow*
grau	*grey*
blau	*blue*
rot	*red*
braun	*brown*

4. Translate the sentences below into **English**.

4.1 Ich trage als Schuluniform eine graue Hose und ein weißes Hemd.

4.2 Ich hasse meine gelbe Schulkrawatte, denn sie ist nicht bequem.

4.3 Die Schüler tragen schwarze Schuhe und weiße Socken.

4.4 In der Schule trägt meine Schwester einen braunen Rock.

4.1 I wear for / as a school uniform grey trousers and a white shirt.

4.2 I hate my yellow school tie, because it is not comfortable.

4.3 The students wear black shoes and white socks.

4.4 My sister wears a brown skirt at school.

! Reminder! Notice the words **einen**, **eine** and **ein** in the sentences above and in Lilian's text about school (Exercise 1). These are indefinite articles, meaning 'a' or 'an'. Their endings change, according to gender and context. The patterns of the changes are similar to those for possessive adjectives (**mein**, **dein**, etc). For more details, see **pages 137 and 139**.

5. Listen to four students (5.1–5.4) describing their uniform. Complete the grid for each student with the adjectives they use, in **English**.

TRACK 16

	trousers / skirt	shirt	jacket	tie	opinion
5.1					
5.2					
5.3					
5.4					

5.1 black / blue / grey / red and grey / not bad

5.2 grey / white / red / black and blue stripes / not comfortable

5.3 blue / grey / blue / red / not practical

5.4 black / white / brown / brown and yellow / ugly

SCHOOL LIFE

Wie ist ein typischer Schultag? ***What is a typical school day like?***

1. Ⓗ Match the questions (1.1–1.8) to the correct answers (A–F).
You will not need all the questions.

1.1 Wie viele Stunden gibt es in einem Schultag?
1.2 Was sind die Nachteile deiner Schule?
1.3 Was macht man in der Stunde?
1.4 Welche Aktivitäten macht man nach der Schule?
1.5 Wie findest du deine Lehrer?
1.6 Welche Schulregeln gibt es?
1.7 Wie ist das Essen in der Kantine?
1.8 Was machst du in der Pause?

A	Sie arbeiten viel und sind sehr hilfsbereit. Manche sind streng und geben uns zu viele Hausaufgaben.
B	Es gibt zu viel Druck, gute Noten bei den Prüfungen zu bekommen. Es ist sehr stressig. Zum Glück gibt es nicht viel Mobbing.
C	Man hört der Erklärung von dem Lehrer zu, macht Aufgaben und lernt zu zweit oder in einer Gruppe. Wir haben interessante Diskussionen.
D	Wir reden oft mit Freunden im Schulhof. Manchmal kaufen wir beim Imbiss etwas zu essen und trinken.
E	Man muss für die Lehrer und die anderen Schüler immer Respekt haben. Man muss auch für den Unterricht pünktlich sein.
F	Die Schule beginnt um acht Uhr. Es gibt drei Stunden vor der Pause. Nach der Pause gibt es zwei Stunden. Man geht in der Mittagspause zur Kantine oder nach Hause.

1.1 F 1.2 B 1.3 C 1.5 A 1.6 E 1.8 D
Questions 1.4 and 1.7 are not matched with an answer. Create your own answers.

2. Ⓗ Using vocabulary from this page to help you, translate these sentences into **German**.

2.1 School starts every day at eight o'clock.
2.2 There is often a lot of bullying.
2.3 I sometimes talk with friends in the school yard.
2.4 A lot of teachers are very strict.
2.5 You always have to be on time.
2.6 I find school quite stressful.

2.1 Die Schule beginnt jeden Tag um acht Uhr. 2.2 Es gibt oft viel Mobbing.
2.3 Ich rede manchmal mit Freunden im Schulhof. 2.4 Viele Lehrer sind sehr streng.
2.5 Man muss immer pünktlich sein. 2.6 Ich finde Schule ziemlich stressig.

! Remember the 'time, manner, place' rule in German. You could practise changing the word order of 2.1, 2.2, 2.3 and 2.5, putting the time phrase first.

Wie ist ein typischer Schultag? continued

3. Listen to these students (3.1–3.4) talking about school. Which **two** aspects of school does each one mention? Is each aspect good or bad, in their opinion?

TRACK 17

A	behaviour	E	rules
B	class activities	F	teachers
C	results	G	timetables
D	facilities	H	uniform

3.1 good D, bad E   3.2 good B, bad A   3.3 good F, bad H   3.4 good C, bad G

Be careful – the opinions won't always come in the order you might expect (the good aspect before the bad one), so listen to the whole of each recording.

4. Prepare answers to questions 1.1–1.8 on **page 36**. Use the ideas and vocabulary on these two pages to help you. Then play the recording, pausing after each question to give your answer.

TRACK 18

If you are a Higher candidate, try to develop your answers as much as possible. Ideas from other pages in Section 1.3 may also be useful.

5. You are writing an article about school life. Write approximately **60 words** in **German**. You must write something about each bullet point. Mention:
   - what you think of your school
   - what you did at school yesterday.

Example answer:

Ich mag meine Schule. Die Stunden für meine Lieblingsfächer sind oft interessant, aber manchmal sind sie auch ein bisschen langweilig. Das Schulgebäude ist modern und sauber und die Lehrer sind immer hilfsbereit und ziemlich lustig.

Ich habe gestern in der Schule Mathe und Englisch gelernt. Ich finde meinen Mathelehrer sehr höflich, aber mein Englischlehrer ist zu streng. Ich habe auch mit Freunden in der Kantine gegessen und meine Hausaufgaben in der Bibliothek gemacht. Es ist nervig, aber nötig!

This question in the exam will have three bullet points and will require a 90 word answer. It will include a bullet point requiring verbs in the future tense, which you will see on **page 39**.

OPTIONS AT AGE 18

Was kann man in der Zukunft machen? *What can you do in the future?*

1. Read this article from a website on education and find the German for the expressions listed below.

Man lernt in der Schule in Deutschland bis man 18 Jahre alt ist. Die Jugendlichen mit 18 Jahren haben viele möglichen Wege: an der Uni zu studieren, eine Ausbildung zu machen oder einen Job zu finden.

In Deutschland gehen manche Jugendliche aufs Gymnasium. Mit 18 Jahren machen sie am Ende der Oberstufe Abitur. Man muss gute Noten in seinen Prüfungen bekommen, um ein Studium an der Uni zu machen. Es gibt viele Kurse, die zu besonderen Karrieren führen.

Wenn man nicht studieren will, kann man auch eine Ausbildung an einem Arbeitsplatz machen. Man arbeitet entweder freiwillig oder man verdient Geld. Man kann auch ins Ausland gehen, um neue Interessen zu finden und die Welt zu sehen.

Gymnasium / Oberstufe / Abitur – *equivalent to grammar school / sixth form / A-Levels*

1.1 lots of different routes
1.2 to study at uni
1.3 to find a job
1.4 to do your A Levels
1.5 studies
1.6 to lead to particular careers
1.7 to do an apprenticeship
1.8 in a workplace
1.9 you earn money
1.10 to travel abroad
1.11 in order to find new interests

1.1 viele möglichen Wege 1.2 an der Uni studieren 1.3 einen Job finden 1.4 Abitur machen 1.5 Studium 1.6 zu besonderen Karrieren führen 1.7 eine Ausbildung machen 1.8 an einem Arbeitsplatz 1.9 man verdient Geld 1.10 ins Ausland gehen 1.11 um neue Interessen zu finden

In texts in both the Foundation and Higher Reading exams, expressions which are hard to interpret in context will be provided for you in a glossary. Try making sense of the meaning of other words, to help you understand the key messages.

2. Adapt the expressions you have found in Exercise 1 to translate the sentences below.

2.1 I am interested in lots of different routes.
2.2 I would like to study at university.
2.3 I can do an apprenticeship.
2.4 I get good grades at school.
2.5 I would like to travel abroad.
2.6 I work, in order to earn money.
2.7 I find A Levels quite difficult.
2.8 I find new interests, in order to find a job.

2.1 Ich interessiere mich für viele möglichen Wege. 2.2 Ich möchte an der Uni studieren. 2.3 Ich kann eine Ausbildung machen. 2.4 Ich bekomme in der Schule gute Noten. 2.5 Ich möchte ins Ausland gehen. 2.6 Ich arbeite, um Geld zu verdienen. 2.7 Ich finde das Abitur ziemlich schwierig. 2.8 Ich finde neue Interessen, um einen Job zu finden.

The future tense

The future tense in German is the equivalent of 'I am going to do something' or 'I will do something'. To form it, you need the correct conjugation of **werden** (*to become*), followed by your main verb in the infinitive.

ich	werde	machen	Ich werde heute meine Hausaufgaben machen. *I'm going to do my homework today.*
du	wirst	studieren	Du wirst Mathe an der Uni studieren. *You're going to study maths at university.*
er/sie/es	wird	finden	Mein Bruder wird morgen einen Job finden. *My brother will find a job tomorrow.*
wir	werden	arbeiten	Wir werden in einem Restaurant arbeiten. *We're going to work in a restaurant.*
ihr	werdet	beginnen	Ihr werdet bald euren Studium beginnen. *You will start your studies soon.*
sie	werden	lernen	Die Schüler werden nächstes Jahr Englisch lernen. *The students will learn English next year.*

! Look at the pattern. The verb **werden** comes as the second idea, while the second verb comes at the end, as an infinitive. Other verb structures, such as **ich möchte** + infinitive, or **man kann** + infinitive, follow the same pattern.

3. Listen to these young people (3.1–3.4) talking about their plans for the future. Which statements are correct? For each person, write **A**, **B** or **A + B**.

TRACK 19

3.1	Katarina is going to	**A** do a science course.	**B** work in a restaurant.
3.2	Jonas is going to	**A** do a new technology course.	**B** do an IT course abroad.
3.3	Sofie is going to	**A** do some more research.	**B** consult her teachers for help.
3.4	Yusuf is going to	**A** do an apprenticeship.	**B** go to university.

3.1 A + B 3.2 B 3.3 A + B 3.4 A + B

4. **H** Translate the following sentences into **German**.

4.1 I am going to do an apprenticeship in IT.

4.2 Are you going to study your favourite subjects at university?

4.3 Leo is going to do some research at the weekend.

4.4 The students are going to do their exams next week.

4.1 Ich werde eine Ausbildung in Informatik machen.
4.2 Wirst du deine Lieblingsfächer an der Uni studieren?
4.3 Leo wird am Wochenende Recherchen machen.
4.4 Die Schüler werden nächste Woche ihre Prüfungen machen.

THE WORLD OF WORK

Welche Berufe interessieren dich? *Which jobs interest you?*

1. Ⓗ Read the statements below and answer the questions in **English**.

Ich suche im Moment Informationen über viele Berufe. Ich glaube, ich interessiere mich am meisten für den Beruf von Anwalt oder von Arzt. Aber für beide muss man sehr lang an der Uni studieren. **Paul**

Für mich ist es am wichtigsten, eine gute Arbeit zu bekommen und ein gutes Gehalt zu verdienen. Arbeit in einem Büro oder einer Bank interessiert mich gar nicht, aber die Wochenenden müssen bestimmt frei bleiben. **Leo**

Mein Beruf darf bestimmt nicht langweilig sein. Es interessiert mich nicht, die gleichen Sachen jeden Tag zu machen! Ich finde Reisen sicherlich attraktiv, besonders ins Ausland. **Anja**

Ich finde die Berufe am interessantesten, die praktisch sind. Mein Lieblingsfach ist Biologie, also interessiert mich vielleicht eine Karriere mit Pflanzen. Gartenarbeit sieht schön aus. Als Bäuerin arbeiten ist auch möglich, denn ich liebe Tiere. **Petra**

1.1 What research is Paul currently doing?
1.2 Why is Paul unsure about his career choices?
1.3 What is most important for Leo?
1.4 What does Leo say about his weekends?
1.5 What does Anja not want in a job? Why?
1.6 What other aspect appeals to her?
1.7 Why is Petra considering gardening?
1.8 Why is Petra considering farming?

der Beruf (-e) *job, career* **der Anwalt / die Anwältin** *lawyer* **der Arzt / die Ärztin** *doctor* **die Pflanze (-n)** *plant* **der Bauer / die Bäuerin** *farmer* **das Gehalt** *salary* **die gleichen Sachen** *the same things*

1.1 research about (many) jobs 1.2 You need to study at university for a long time. 1.3 find a good job / earn a good wage 1.4 Weekends must be free. 1.5 not do the same things every day, get bored 1.6 travelling, especially abroad 1.7 Her favourite subject is biology / She is interested in plants. 1.8 She loves animals.

\+ Use **am** + adjective + -**sten** to say 'the most ... (thing)'. See more superlatives on **page 143**.

am wichtigsten	*the most important*	am liebsten	*the most preferable*
am interessantesten	*the most interesting*	am schönsten	*the nicest*
am besten	*the best*	am schlimmsten	*the worst*

Die Vor- und Nachteile von Berufen — *The pluses and minuses of jobs*

2. Read the list of pros and cons of jobs (A–E) and match them to the correct jobs (1–5).

A	⊕ viele Ferien ⊖ viel Vorbereitung	1	*doctor*
B	⊕ kostenloses Essen ⊖ unhöfliche Kunden	2	*postal worker*
C	⊕ billigere Preise ⊖ ganzen Tag beschäftigt	3	*teacher*
D	⊕ viel Bewegung ⊖ aggressive Hunde	4	*shop assistant*
E	⊕ Menschen helfen ⊖ langes Studium	5	*waiter / waitress*

die Vorbereitung *preparation* **beschäftigt** *busy, occupied* **die Bewegung** *exercise*

A3 B5 C4 D2 E1

3. **H** Listen to these people (3.1–3.4). Which job does each one do? Select the correct letter.

TRACK 20

3.1	**A** lawyer	**B** bank employee	**C** journalist
3.2	**A** police officer	**B** politician	**C** doctor
3.3	**A** actor	**B** film director	**C** screenwriter
3.4	**A** artist	**B** fashion designer	**C** musician

3.1 B 3.2 C 3.3 A 3.4 B

4. **H** Translate the sentences into **English**.

4.1 Ich möchte als Chef für eine große Technikfirma arbeiten.
4.2 Technologie ist faszinierend.
4.3 Ich möchte mehr über Computer lernen.
4.4 Ich könnte Menschen mit technischen Schwierigkeiten helfen.
4.5 In dieser Industrie gibt es glücklicherweise viel Arbeit.

4.1 I would like to work as the head / boss of a big technology company. 4.2 Technology is fascinating. 4.3 I would like to learn more about computers. 4.4 I could help people with technical difficulties. 4.5 In this industry / sector there is fortunately / luckily a lot of work.

PREPARING FOR WORK

Arbeit suchen — *Looking for work*

1. Read these three adverts and decide which of the following requirements they each mention. Make **three** lists, for adverts A, B and C.

A

Reisebüro Echt

Bitte schicken Sie uns eine E-Mail, wenn Sie:

- Arbeitserfahrung im Flughafen haben,
- Englisch und Deutsch sprechen,
- mit Kollegen ins Ausland fahren wollen,
- ruhig und geduldig mit Kunden sind.

B

Eine Arbeitsstelle am **Hotel See**

Sind Sie eine Person, die:

- höflich ist?
- unter Druck arbeiten kann?
- an Wochenenden arbeiten kann?
- sich gut mit anderen Menschen versteht?

Finden Sie mehr Informationen auf unserer Webseite.

C

Kino Stern braucht eine/-n Mitarbeiter/-in

Man muss:

- sich für Filme interessieren,
- technische Kompetenzen haben,
- in einem Team arbeiten können,
- hilfsbereit und kreativ sein.

1.1 can work weekends
1.2 good tech knowledge
1.3 airport experience
1.4 able to work in a team
1.5 able to work under pressure
1.6 willing to travel
1.7 calm and patient
1.8 speaks English
1.9 helpful
1.10 polite
1.11 gets on with people
1.12 interested in film

A: 1.3, 1.6, 1.7, 1.8 B: 1.1, 1.5, 1.10, 1.11 C: 1.2, 1.4, 1.9, 1.12

! Yet another **sie** pronoun! In this case, **Sie** (always with a capital S) is the formal version of 'you', singular and plural. In advert A, notice that the verb conjugations for **Sie** are the same as for **sie** (*they*). Different verb conjugations are used for the singular **sie** (*she / a person who ...*).

2. **H** Julian has an interview. His friends message him with advice.
Who gives these pieces of advice? Answer the questions, using the initial of the friend.

2.1 Dress smartly.
2.2 Get there with time to spare.
2.3 Research the company.
2.4 Have a practice interview.
2.5 Go to bed early the night before.
2.6 Think up some questions to ask the company.
2.7 Think about the questions they will ask you.
2.8 Ask for the teachers' help.
2.9 Do not leave the house late.
2.10 My brother could help.

T – Thomas
Davor solltest du im Internet Informationen über die Firma finden. Du solltest auch darüber nachdenken, welche Fragen du der Firma stellen möchtest.

M – Maria
Du musst pünktlich sein. Wenn man spät das Haus verlässt und nicht genug Zeit hat, ist das zu viel Druck.

E – Elisabeth
Was wirst du tragen? Mein Bruder hat eine elegante Jacke. Vielleicht kann er dir helfen.

K – Karl
Versuch, deine Antworten vor dem Vorstellungsgespräch vorzubereiten. Deine Lehrer können dich unterstützen.

D – David
Du kannst im Internet suchen, was es für typische Fragen geben wird. Du musst für alles bereit sein!

O – Omar
Du brauchst acht Stunden Schlaf, also solltest du die Nacht davor früh ins Bett gehen.

2.1 E 2.2 M 2.3 T 2.4 K 2.5 O 2.6 T 2.7 D 2.8 K 2. 9 M 2.10 E

3. Translate these sentences into **German**.
3.1 As a person, I am intelligent and helpful.
3.2 I can work at weekends.
3.3 I like working in a team.
3.4 I speak German and English.
3.5 I am interested in travel and also theatre.

3.1 Ich bin als Person intelligent und hilfsbereit. 3.2 Ich kann an Wochenenden arbeiten.
3.3 Ich arbeite gern in einem Team. 3.4 Ich spreche Deutsch und Englisch.
3.5 Ich interessiere mich für Reisen und auch Theater.

EDUCATION AND WORK

Zusammensetzen | *Putting it all together*

1. **H** Mathias has moved house and is about to start a new school. He emails his friend. Read the text and answer the questions in **English**.

> Hallo Reinwald!
>
> Gestern habe ich meine neue Hauptschule besucht. Die Schule fängt am nächsten Montag wieder an, aber es war gut, das Schulgebäude zu sehen und einige Lehrer kennenzulernen. Es ist viel größer als meine letzte Schule – hoffentlich werde ich mich nicht verlieren – aber es ist modern und sauber. Am besten ist, dass die Schule nicht so weit von meinem Haus liegt, also wird es sehr einfach sein, morgens zu Fuß zur Schule zu gehen.
>
> Im Allgemeinen sind die Lehrer nett, außer dem Lehrer für Geschichte. Er war zu ernst für mich! Ich glaube, er wird streng sein.
>
> Am schlimmsten ist, dass ich leider keine Schüler kenne. Das heißt, niemand wird mit mir in der Kantine oder in den Stunden sitzen. Das wird ein bisschen unangenehm sein.
>
> **Mathias**

1.1 When does the new term start?

1.2 Why did he visit the school? (Give **two** details)

1.3 Why does the size of the school worry him?

1.4 What two things did he notice about the school building?

1.5 How will he get to school and why?

1.6 What was his impression of most of the teachers?

1.7 What did he think about the history teacher?

1.8 What does Mathias say is the worst thing about starting a new school?

1.9 Look at the last line. What do you think **unangenehm** means?

A confident **B** bullied **C** unpleasant

1.1 Next Monday. 1.2 To see the building and meet some teachers. 1.3 He thinks he'll get lost. 1.4 It's modern and clean. 1.5 He'll walk; it's not far from his house. 1.6 They're nice. 1.7 He was too serious; he will be strict. 1.8 Not knowing any other students. 1.9 C

2. Listen to these young people (2.1–2.4) talking about their current school. Are their opinions positive (**P**), negative (**N**) or both positive and negative (**P + N**)?

TRACK 21

2.1 P 2.2 N 2.3 P + N 2.4 P + N

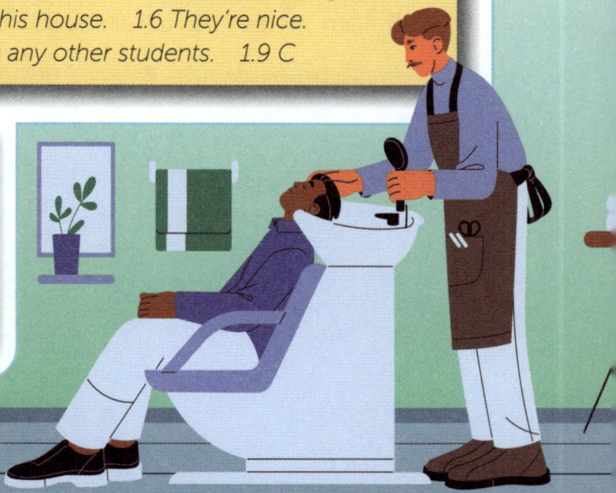

Zusammensetzen continued

Dictation

3. Ⓗ You will hear five sentences, repeated three times. Write them down in **German**. (Note that on the Foundation Ⓕ paper, there are only four sentences.)

TRACK 22

3.1 Ich habe Stunden für Geschichte und Erdkunde. 3.2 Die Schüler sind dieses Jahr unhöflich. 3.3 Die Pause beginnt um elf Uhr. 3.4 Ich möchte Journalist oder Autor werden. 3.5 Ich will Jugendliche unterstützen.

4. Ⓕ Complete each sentence with the correct word.

4.1 Mein Lieblingsfach ________________ Naturwissenschaften. (**A** sind **B** ist **C** wäre)

4.2 Nächstes Jahr ________________ ich weiterstudieren. (**A** werde **B** wird **C** werden)

4.3 Es ist ______________ wichtig, sich für einen Beruf zu interessieren. (**A** nicht **B** besonders)

4.4 Ich möchte an der Uni ________________ studieren. (**A** Note **B** Ausbildung **C** Literatur)

4.5 Heute Nachmittag muss ich meine Hausaufgaben ________________ .
(**A** gemacht **B** machen **C** mache)

4.1 B 4.2 A 4.3 B 4.4 C 4.5 B

Photo card

5. Look at the two photos and make notes about what you can say about them. Then set a timer and talk about the content of the photos.
Foundation Ⓕ students have **one minute** to talk and Higher Ⓗ students have a **minute and a half**. Listen to the recording to hear a student talking about the photos.

Photo 1

Photo 2

TRACK 23

6. You are writing to a German friend about school and your plans next year. Write approximately **90 words** in **German**. You must write something about each bullet point.
Mention:
- life at school
- your favourite subject
- what you plan to study next year

Example answer: Ich mag meine Schule und fast alle Fächer sind interessant, außer Mathe. Ich bekomme schlechte Noten, denn ich verstehe meinen Lehrer nicht und er ist gar nicht geduldig mit mir. Mein Lieblingsfach ist Sport, denn ich bin in vielen Sportarten schon sehr gut. Ich mag Basketball, aber am liebsten mache ich Leichtathletik. Nächstes Jahr muss man drei Fächer zum Abitur wählen. Ich werde Sport (natürlich!), Psychologie und Englisch lernen. Das ist ideal, um eine Karriere als Trainer zu bekommen, oder Arbeit im Ausland zu finden.

KEY VOCABULARY

Students are expected to know 1200 items of vocabulary for Foundation tier and a further 500 for Higher tier. This list has some of the key vocabulary for Theme 1, but there are many more words listed in the AQA specification and in an interactive spreadsheet on the AQA website.

arbeiten (an + ***noun*****)**	*to work (on + noun)*
heiraten	*to marry*
unterstützen	*to support*
sich mit + Person verstehen	*to get on with + person*
essen	*to eat*
kochen	*to cook*
schlafen	*to sleep*
trinken	*to drink*
vermeiden	*to avoid*
organisieren	*to organise*
reisen	*to travel*
träumen	*to dream*
die Beziehung	*relationship*
die Kommunikation	*communication*
die Liebe	*love*
das Gefühl	*feeling*
der Typ	*bloke*
die Bewegung	*movement, motion*
die Gesundheit	*health*
die Krankheit	*illness*
der Körper	*body*
das Leben	*life*
die Kleidung	*clothing*
die Welt	*world*
der Freund / die Freundin	*friend*
der Unterricht	*lesson, class*
das Mobbing	*bullying*
erfolgreich	*successful*
kulturell	*cultural*
ledig	*single*
allein	*alone*
gefährlich	*dangerous*
sportlich	*sporty, athletic*

EXAMINATION PRACTICE

People and lifestyle – Reading

H You read a blog about family life on a German website.

Ich glaube, die Beziehung zwischen Eltern und Kindern ist jetzt nicht so eng als sie früher war. Ich denke, Eltern haben eine allgemein positive Einstellung und sind eigentlich entspannt. Für mich sind sie mehr wie Freunde, oder vielleicht ältere Geschwister. Die Jugendlichen haben in ihrem sozialen Leben mehr Freiheit. Das heißt, ihre Eltern sind heutzutage nicht so streng als früher. Am schlimmsten für Jugendliche ist das Problem von Geld. Familien müssen jetzt viel mehr ihre Kinder für länger unterstützen, denn die Jugendlichen haben wenige Chancen, unabhängig zu werden. Viele junge Leute wohnen normalerweise bei ihren Eltern zu Hause, bis sie dreißig Jahre alt oder älter sind.

die Einstellung – *attitude, outlook*

Complete these sentences. Write the letter for the correct option.

01 The parent–child relationship ...
A is difficult because of the generation gap. **B** has changed in recent years.
C is not so different from how it used to be. [1 mark]

02 These days, parents ...
A are more easy-going. **B** work longer hours. **C** choose to have fewer children. [1 mark]

03 Young people generally ...
A are well disciplined. **B** have more freedom. **C** respect their parents. [1 mark]

04 On the other hand, young people lack ...
A financial independence. **B** drive and initiative. **C** resilience. [1 mark]

05 Many young people ...
A start a family at a later age. **B** look for a house to share. **C** stay at home for several years. [1 mark]

You see an online forum where some Austrian students are discussing their lifestyle.
Who mentions what? Write **M** for Mila, **G** for Gisele, or **M + G** for Mila and Gisele. [6 marks]

Ich habe morgens keinen Hunger. Ich esse kein Frühstück und meine Mutter wird dann mit mir böse. Ich bringe zwei Stück Obst mit zur Schule und esse sie in der Pause. Ich gehe zu Fuß in die Schule und auch nach Hause. Es dauert dreißig Minuten. **Mila**

Ich stehe nicht gern früh auf und normalerweise ziehe ich meine Kleidung an und gehe dann sofort in die Schule. In der Pause kaufe ich in der Schulkantine etwas zu essen und eine Flasche Wasser. Ich bin sehr sportlich und spiele in vielen Mannschaften, schwimme und fahre jeden Tag mit dem Rad zur Schule. **Gisele**

06 How they get to school
07 Skipping breakfast
08 Eating fruit
09 Having a drink
10 Doing a lot of walking
11 Going swimming

People and lifestyle – Listening

01–06 You are listening to the presenters on German breakfast TV announcing what is on the show. Which feature of the programme do they each mention?
Write the correct letter for each announcement (01–06). [6 marks] TRACK 24

Announcement 01 ____________________

Announcement 02 ____________________

Announcement 03 ____________________

Announcement 04 ____________________

Announcement 05 ____________________

Announcement 06 ____________________

A	Choosing your options
B	Cooking vegan food
C	Exercising with friends
D	Friendship award
E	Staying healthy for older people
F	Local job opportunities
G	Study support
H	Solving sleep problems

Ⓗ Listen to Ingrid talking to her grandmother on the phone and telling her about her studies. Complete the sentences in **English**. [5 marks] TRACK 25

07 Ingrid says that last year, she and her classmates ______________________________ .

08 If they didn't do PE in school, ____ .

09 The literature teacher gives them ____ .

10 During the Kiel trip, the class will have the opportunity to try out ______________________________
and ____ .

Ⓗ Dictation

TRACK 26

11–15 You will now hear **five** short sentences.

Listen carefully and, using your knowledge of German sounds, write down in **German** exactly what you hear for each sentence.

You will hear each sentence **three** times: the first time as a full sentence, the second time in short sections and the third time again as a full sentence.

Use your knowledge of German sounds and grammar to make sure that what you have written makes sense. Check carefully that your spelling is accurate. [10 marks]

(Note that, on the Foundation paper, there are only four sentences.)

People and lifestyle – Speaking

Role play

Plan what you are going to say in this role play, taking into account the number of details you will need. Remember to use a verb in each response.

TRACK 27

Then play the recording, pausing after each question or statement so you can give your response. (F This is in the style of a Foundation tier role play.)
When you see this **– ? –** you will have to ask a question. [10 marks]

You are talking to your Austrian friend.

01 Say what your friend looks like. (Give **one** detail.)

02 Say why you get on with your friend. (Give **one** detail.)

03 Say what you think of your school. (Give **one** opinion.)

04 Say what your favourite subject is. (Give **one** detail.)

? 05 Ask your friend a question about their family.

---

06 H **Read aloud** the following passage and then answer the questions in the recording.
This is a Higher tier task. [5 + 10 marks]

Es ist manchmal schwer, gesund zu bleiben. Jetzt gibt es Sportspiele und Initiativen für jüngere Menschen. Heute kochen mehr Leute zu Hause. Das ist natürlich besser für den Körper. Manche Jugendliche essen immer noch zu viel Fastfood. Sie brauchen Hilfe von ihren Eltern oder anderen Erwachsenen.

TRACK 28

Photo card

07 Look at the two photos and prepare ideas on what to say about them. Remember to say something about **both** photos and to talk for one minute F or one and a half minutes H. Then listen to the recording to hear an example of what could be said. [5 marks]

TRACK 29

Photo 1

Photo 2

08 Now answer the recorded questions for the unprepared conversation on the theme. [20 marks]

TRACK 30

People and lifestyle – Writing

01 Translate the following sentences into **English**. [10 marks]

01.1 Ich bin sehr glücklich, Ingrid als Freundin zu haben.

01.2 Sie ist sehr lieb und hört mir zu.

01.3 Ein guter Freund ist immer für dich da.

01.4 Wir teilen unsere Interessen und lachen zusammen.

01.5 Sie ist sehr ehrlich und lügt nie.

In the exam, the translation into English is the last question on the Reading paper.

02 Translate the following sentences into **German**. [10 marks]

02.1 He has brown hair and he wears glasses.

02.2 Sometimes I fight with my brother.

02.3 I am going to study three subjects next year.

02.4 You do not have to study all subjects.

02.5 I hate our uniform – it is very ugly.

03 You are writing an article about healthy lifestyle.
Write approximately **90 words** in **German**.
You must write something about each bullet point.

Mention:

- some healthy meals that you like
- the exercise you will do next week
- something healthy that you did last week. [15 marks]

Transfer your learning from one part of the theme to another, e.g. the future tense in Topic 1.3 (page 39, future studies) to this context of healthy lifestyle from Topic 1.2.

04 **H** You are writing a post for an online magazine about education and work.
Write approximately **150 words** in **German**.
You must write something about each bullet point.

Mention:

- a typical day in your school
- your plans for education and work in the future. [25 marks]

TOPICS FOR THEME 2

Popular culture

Specification coverage

Topic 1 Free-time activities

Topic 2 Customs, festivals and celebrations

Topic 3 Celebrity culture

Information about the four papers for Foundation Ⓕ and Higher Ⓗ tiers:

Paper 1 – Listening

Written exam:
35 minutes Ⓕ, 45 minutes Ⓗ
40 marks Ⓕ, 50 marks Ⓗ
25% of GCSE

The recording is controlled by the invigilator with built-in repetitions and pauses.

Each exam includes 5 minutes' reading time at the start of the question paper before the listening material is played and 2 minutes at the end of the recording to check your work.

Section A – Listening comprehension questions in English, to be answered in English or non-verbally (Ⓕ 32 marks, Ⓗ 40 marks).

Section B – Dictation where students transcribe 4 sentences (Ⓕ 8 marks) or 5 sentences (Ⓗ 10 marks).

Paper 3 – Reading

Written exam: 45 minutes Ⓕ, 1 hour Ⓗ
50 marks, 25% of GCSE

Section A – Reading comprehension questions in English, to be answered in English or non-verbally (40 marks).

Section B – Translation from German into English, minimum of 35 words Ⓕ or 50 words Ⓗ (10 marks).

Paper 2 – Speaking

Non-exam assessment (NEA):
7–9 minutes Ⓕ or 10–12 minutes Ⓗ +
15 minutes' supervised preparation time
50 marks, 25% of GCSE

Role play – 10 marks, 1-1.5 minutes. Ⓕ Ⓗ

Reading aloud passage and short conversation – 15 marks.
Recommended time 2-2.5 minutes Ⓕ and 3-3.5 minutes Ⓗ.
Minimum 35 words Ⓕ and minimum 50 words Ⓗ.

Photo card discussion (two photos) – 25 marks.
Photo card discussion time:
4-5 minutes Ⓕ and 6-7 minutes Ⓗ.

Paper 4 – Writing

Written exam: 1 hour 10 minutes Ⓕ,
1 hour 15 minutes Ⓗ
50 marks, 25% of GCSE

Set of three short writing tasks. Ⓕ only. 25 marks.

Translation of sentences from English into German, minimum 35 words Ⓕ, or 50 words Ⓗ (10 marks).

Produce a piece of writing in response to three compulsory bullet points, approximately 90 words in total. Choose from two questions (15 marks). Ⓕ Ⓗ

Open-ended writing task.
Two compulsory bullet points, approximately 150 words in total. Choose from two questions. (25 marks). Ⓗ only.

ACTIVITIES AT HOME

Was machst du gern zu Hause? *What do you like doing at home?*

essen	*to eat*
fernsehen	*to watch TV*
Musik hören	*to listen to music*
online einkaufen	*to shop online*
kochen	*to cook*
Schuhe kaufen	*to buy shoes*
ein Buch lesen	*to read a book*
Freunden schreiben	*to write to friends*
singen	*to sing*
Videospiele spielen	*to play video games*
Sendungen streamen	*to stream programmes*

The present tense – irregular verbs

Some verbs are slightly different in the present tense in the forms for **du** and **er/sie/es** – there is a vowel change that you need to remember. The pattern for the other forms (**ich**, **wir**, **sie** plural) stays closer to the spelling of the verb infinitive.

	Regular forms	Irregular forms with vowel change
essen *to eat*	ich esse, wir essen, sie essen	du isst, er/sie/es isst
fernsehen *to watch TV*	ich sehe fern, wir sehen fern, sie sehen fern	du siehst fern, er/sie/es sieht fern
laufen *to run*	ich laufe, wir laufen, sie laufen	du läufst, er/sie/es läuft
lesen *to read*	ich lese, wir lesen, sie lesen	du liest, er/sie/es liest
schlafen *to sleep*	ich schlafe, wir schlafen, sie schlafen	du schläfst, er/sie/es schläft

Find a list of irregular verbs in the verb tables on **pages 163-166**.

1. Listen to Victoria describing the activities of different members (1.1–1.5) of her family. Who is she talking about and what are they doing? Write the answers in **English**.

TRACK 31

2. Put the verbs in brackets into the correct form of the present tense.

   2.1 Was ____________ (essen) du am Wochenende zu Hause?

   2.2 Ich sehe nicht oft fern, aber mein Bruder ____________ (sehen) oft im Wohnzimmer fern.

   2.3 Meine Schwester ____________ (lesen) ein Buch oder die Zeitung.

   2.4 Meine Eltern und ich laufen zusammen, aber meine Großmutter ____________ (laufen) nie.

1.1 brother – writing to friends 1.2 parents – cooking 1.3 sisters – watching TV
1.4 grandmother – reading a book 1.5 herself/Victoria – shopping online

2.1 isst 2.2 sieht 2.3 liest 2.4 läuft

Adjectives to describe activities

aktiv	*active*	**kreativ**	*creative*
beliebt	*popular*	**musikalisch**	*musical*
bequem	*comfortable*	**offen**	*open*
einfach	*easy*	**ruhig**	*calm, quiet*
entspannend	*relaxing*	**schnell**	*quick*
gefährlich	*dangerous*	**schwierig**	*difficult*
gesund	*healthy*	**sportlich**	*sporty*

+ Look at the sentence beginning **Heute Abend** in Exercise 3 **below**. It's a good example of someone talking about the future but using the present tense, together with a future time marker, meaning 'this evening'.

3. Read Olaf's description of what his friends are doing and answer the questions.

Meine Freunde und ich machen gern viele unterschiedliche Aktivitäten zusammen zu Hause. Mein Freund Jens findet neue Kleidung online und kauft neue Schuhe und T-Shirts, die bequem und beliebt sind. Meine Freundin Clara hört lieber im Garten Musik, denn es ist für sie entspannend, und sie ist als Person sehr ruhig. Aber ich bin als Person sportlich. In den Schulferien spiele ich normalerweise Fußball, um aktiv zu sein. Heute lese ich ein Buch für meinen Englischunterricht. Ich finde es schwierig! Heute Abend streamen meine Freunde und ich einen Film oder eine neue Sendung. Ich esse viel Popcorn, aber Clara isst keins. Sie isst gesund.

Olaf

3.1 Why is Jens online?

3.2 Which **two** adjectives does Olaf use to describe Jens' activity?

3.3 Why does Clara listen to music?

3.4 When does Olaf play football?

3.5 What is Olaf doing today? What does he think of it?

3.6 What is Clara not doing this evening and why?

4. Read aloud the passage and then listen to the recording to check your pronunciation.

TRACK 32

Ich habe gestern zwei Stunden lang gelesen. Ich mag Bücher, aber ich mache lieber Sport, denn ich möchte aktiv bleiben. Eine gute Freundin von mir heißt Amelia. Sie ist lustig und lieb, aber sie schläft oft oder sie sieht fern.

5. Use the texts in Exercises 3 and 4 to help you write **five** sentences about things you and your friends do at home.

3.1 Buying new clothes / Buying new shoes and t-shirts. 3.2 Comfortable and popular.
3.3 Music is relaxing / She is a quiet person. 3.4 During the school holidays.
3.5 Reading a book for English, finds it difficult. 3.6 Not eating popcorn, as she eats healthily.

5. Model sentences: Ich mache jeden Tag im Garten Sport.
Mein Freund hört jeden Tag Musik. Meine Freunde und ich essen oft zusammen Pizza.
Heute Abend mache ich meine Hausaufgaben für meinen Deutschunterricht.
Heute streame ich einen Film, aber meine Freundin Sara macht es nicht gern.

ACTIVITIES OUTSIDE THE HOME

Aktivitäten mit deinen Freunden | *Activities with your friends*

Useful vocabulary

ein Match gewinnen	*to win a match*
auf ein Konzert gehen	*to go to a concert*
lachen	*to laugh*
auf eine Party gehen	*to go to a party*
joggen gehen	*to go jogging*
ins Kino gehen	*to go to the cinema*
Sport treiben/machen	*to do sport*
tanzen gehen	*to go dancing*
Geburtstag feiern	*to celebrate a birthday*
mit Freunden ausgehen	*to go out with friends*
spazieren gehen	*to go for a walk*
einkaufen gehen	*to go shopping*
in (den) Urlaub fahren	*to go on holiday*
Basketball spielen	*to play basketball*

Ⓗ The imperfect (simple past)

Use the imperfect or simple past tense to say something you did in the past and are no longer doing. The regular endings for this tense are:

	spielen
-te	ich spielte
-test	du spieltest
-te	er/sie/es spielte
-ten	wir spielten
-tet	ihr spieltet
-ten	sie spielten

Some common verbs have a vowel change:

essen – ich aß
fernsehen – ich sah fern
lesen – ich las
gehen – ich ging
laufen – ich lief
fahren – ich fuhr
schwimmen – ich schwamm
bleiben – ich blieb

For more irregular forms of this tense, see **pages 163-166**.

1. Ⓗ Put the verbs in brackets into the correct form of the imperfect/simple past tense.

In den Sommerferien 1.1 __________ (machen) ich viele Aktivitäten mit meinen Freunden. Meine Freunde und ich 1.2 __________ (gehen) in die Stadtmitte und 1.3 __________ (kaufen) Kleidung. Nachmittags 1.4 __________ (schwimmen) wir im Schwimmbad. Wir 1.5 __________ (essen) abends zusammen und danach 1.6 _______ (tanzen) wir auf einer Party. Manchmal 1.7 __________ (bleiben) ich zu Hause und 1.8 __________ (sehen) fern.

1.1 machte 1.2 gingen 1.3 kauften 1.4 schwammen 1.5 aßen 1.6 tanzten 1.7 blieb 1.8 sah

Aktivitäten mit deinen Freunden continued

2. Translate the sentences into **German**.

   Ⓕ + Ⓗ Foundation and Higher candidates can use the perfect tense for the verbs here.

   Ⓗ Higher candidates only, use a mix of perfect and imperfect tenses to add variety.

   2.1 I went for a walk with my dog this morning.

   2.2 I played guitar in a concert last week.

   2.3 Last year I went on holiday with my parents.

   2.4 My friends and I went to the cinema last Saturday.

   2.5 Last month my sister celebrated her birthday.

2.1 Ich bin heute Morgen mit meinem Hund spazieren gegangen. 2.2 Ich habe letzte Woche auf einem Konzert Gitarre gespielt. 2.3 Ich bin letztes Jahr mit meinen Eltern in (den) Urlaub gefahren. 2.4 Meine Freunde und ich sind letzten Samstag ins Kino gegangen. 2.5 Letzten Monat hat meine Schwester ihren Geburtstag gefeiert.

\+ For extra practice, rewrite them putting the time phrase first, e.g. **Heute Morgen bin ich ...**

Photo card

3. Look at the two photos and make notes about what you can say about them. Then set a timer and talk about the content of the photos.

   Foundation Ⓕ students have **one minute** to talk and Higher Ⓗ students have a **minute and a half**. Listen to the recording to hear a student talking about the photos.

TRACK 33

Photo 1

Photo 2

\+ Listen to the track for the photo cards and write out as many of the key details as you can. Practise saying these answers aloud and make a note of the most useful ones. These may help you to answer the four questions after the photo card in the exam.

TV AND CINEMA

Welche Filme siehst du gern? *What films do you like watching?*

1. Read what these people like to watch and why. Find the German for the phrases listed.

Ich sehe gern Seifenopern, denn sie unterhalten gut.

Ich gehe am liebsten ins Kino und sehe Filme für Kinder.

Kochsendungen sind sehr beliebt und helfen, mich zu entspannen.

Ich sehe nicht gern Dokumentarfilme, denn sie sind oft zu lang. Manchmal kann man etwas lernen.

Ich sehe gern Sportsendungen und die Matchs mit den besten Mannschaften.

Mein Lieblingsschauspieler ist fantastisch und spielt die Hauptrolle in meiner Lieblingssendung.

1.1 I like to watch 1.2 entertain 1.3 they help me to relax 1.4 documentaries
1.5 often too long 1.6 to learn something 1.7 the games 1.8 the main role

1.1 ich sehe gern 1.2 unterhalten 1.3 sie helfen, mich zu entspannen 1.4 Dokumentarfilme 1.5 oft zu lang 1.6 etwas lernen 1.7 die Matchs 1.8 die Hauptrolle

Saying 'because' – weil or denn

The conjunction **weil** means 'because'. When you use it, the verb does not follow straight on after the pronoun, but instead goes to the end of the clause. Compare the German and English here:

Ich sehe gern Dokumentarfilme, weil sie interessant sind. *I like watching documentary films because they are interesting.*

If you use **denn** instead, the verb stays in its place. So the meaning of the sentence stays the same:

Ich sehe gern Dokumentarfilme, denn sie sind interessant.

2. Translate the sentences into **German**. Write them out **twice**: with **denn**, then with **weil**.

2.1 I do not like to watch soap operas, because they are not interesting.

2.2 I love sports programmes, because I am active and sporty.

2.3 I like watching TV series most of all, because they are fun.

2.4 I like streaming programmes, because there are a lot of interesting topics.

2.1 Ich sehe nicht gern Seifenopern, denn sie sind nicht interessant. / weil sie nicht interessant sind. 2.2 Ich liebe Sportsendungen, denn ich bin aktiv und sportlich. / weil ich aktiv und sportlich bin. 2.3 Ich sehe am liebsten Serien, denn sie machen Spaß. / weil sie Spaß machen. 2.4 Ich streame gern Sendungen, denn es gibt viele interessante Themen. / weil es viele interessante Themen gibt.

3. Match up the German and the English for these frequency expressions.

1	ab und zu
2	abends
3	am Wochenende
4	einmal pro Woche
5	fast
6	immer
7	jeden Tag
8	kaum
9	manchmal
10	montags
11	nie
12	wenigstens

A	*never*
B	*hardly*
C	*once a week*
D	*at least*
E	*at the weekend*
F	*now and then*
G	*sometimes*
H	*almost*
I	*on Mondays*
J	*in the evenings*
K	*every day*
L	*always*

1F 2J 3E 4C 5H 6L 7K 8B 9G 10I 11A 12D

Role play

4. Ⓗ Plan what you are going to say in this role play, taking into account the number of details you will need. Then play the recording, pausing after each question or statement so you can give your response.
When you see this **–?–** you will have to ask a question.

TRACK 34

4.1 Say what you do with your friends at the weekend. (Give **two** details.)

4.2 Give your opinion about going to the cinema and say why you think that. (Give **one opinion** and **one reason**.)

4.3 Say what you did at home last Saturday. (Give **two** details.)

4.4 Say when you like to listen to music.

? 4.5 Ask your friend a question about their free time.

5. Prepare **four** sentences, each describing an activity you do in your free time and how often you do it. Read them out, then hide your notes and say them from memory.

ACTIVITIES IN THE PAST, PRESENT AND FUTURE

In der Vergangenheit, im Präsens und in Zukunft — *In the past, present and future*

In order to achieve higher marks in your speaking and writing, you need to demonstrate that you can use three different time frames.

Remember that time frame is not the same as tense. For example, in this sentence: **Ich hoffe, nach Deutschland zu fahren** *I hope to go to Germany*, even though the verb is in the present tense, the sentence expresses a future time frame.

Equally, **Ich spiele seit zwei Jahren Gitarre** *I have been playing the guitar for two years* is a past time frame, even though the verb is in the present tense.

Using expressions like this, as well as a variety of tenses, can help you increase the complexity of your German.

Here are some useful time expressions you can use when writing across three time frames.

Past	
vor zwei Jahren	*two years ago*
letztes Wochenende	*last weekend*
im letzten Urlaub	*on my last holiday*
als Kind	*as a child*

Present	
normalerweise	*normally*
immer	*always*
jedes Wochenende	*every weekend*
freitags	*on Fridays*
morgens	*in the mornings*

Future	
nächstes Jahr	*next year*
nächstes Wochenende	*next weekend*
im nächsten Urlaub	*on my next holiday*
in fünf Jahren	*in five years*
wenn ich älter bin	*when I am older*
wenn ich zwanzig Jahre alt bin	*when I am twenty years old*
irgendwann	*sometime, some day*

1. Ⓕ Choose the correct option for the gap in each sentence. This type of exercise appears in the Foundation writing exam only.

1.1 Ich ______________ nächstes Wochenende mit meinen Freunden aus.
gegangen **werde** **gehe**

1.2 Ich ______________ jeden Tag um sieben Uhr.
frühstücken **frühstückte** **frühstücke**

1.3 Ich ______________ irgendwann in der Zukunft ein Haus ______________ .
werde ... kaufen **habe ... gekauft** **kaufen**

1.4 Ich ______________ immer eine Schuluniform.
tragen **getragen** **trage**

2. Put the verbs in brackets in the correct **ich** (*I*) form in the appropriate tense. Then translate the sentences into **English**.

2.1 Ich ______________ letztes Wochenende in einem Restaurant ______________ (essen).

2.2 Ich ______________ (treiben) jedes Wochenende Sport.

2.3 Ich ______________ (studieren) seit vier Jahren an der Uni.

2.4 Ich ______________ (sehen) sonntags zu Hause fern.

2.5 Ich ______________ in einer Musikgruppe Gitarre ______________ (spielen), wenn ich älter bin.

2.6 Ich ______________ im letzten Urlaub für meine Freunde Geschenke ______________ (kaufen).

2.7 Ich ______________ meinen Freund vor zwei Jahren in Südösterreich ______________ (besuchen).

1.1 gehe 1.2 frühstücke 1.3 werde ... kaufen 1.4 trage

2.1 habe ... gegessen – Last weekend I ate in a restaurant. 2.2 treibe – I do sport every weekend. 2.3 studiere – I have been studying at uni for four years. 2.4 sehe – I watch TV on Sundays at home. 2.5 werde ... spielen – I am going to play guitar in a band when I am older. 2.6 habe ... gekauft – I bought gifts for my friends on my last holiday. 2.7 habe ... besucht – I visited my friend in south Austria two years ago.

Dictation

TRACK 35

3. Listen to five sentences and write them down in **German**. You will hear them once in full, a second time in sections, and once again in full the third time through.

3.1 Ich habe letztes Jahr in einer Mannschaft Fußball gespielt.
3.2 Ich mache gern Videos in meinem Garten.
3.3 Ich finde Dokumentarfilme kreativ.
3.4 Spazieren ist gut für die Gesundheit.
3.5 Ich sehe nicht gern Actionfilme.

WHAT OTHER PEOPLE DO

Was macht deine Familie? *What do your family do?*

To add complexity to your writing, include some verbs in forms for other persons, not just 'I'. For example, don't just write about what you did last weekend, say what your friends did too.

Another way of adding complexity is by being confident with using some irregular verbs, e.g. those that change the vowel in the **er**/**sie**/**es** form, or that have an irregular past participle.

1. Read these comments describing what people do, did or will do in their free time.

Mein Bruder hat immer mit Freunden im Park Fußball gespielt, als er Kind war, aber ich bin lieber zu Hause geblieben. Ich treibe jetzt mehr Sport. **Sebastian**

Meine Eltern sind vor zwei Wochen ins Kino und danach ins Restaurant gegangen, um einen Geburtstag zu feiern. Sie waren glücklich, denn sie essen gern japanisches Essen. **Ingrid**

Ich spiele am Computer, wenn ich zu Hause bin. Mein Bruder muss mir manchmal mit den Hausaufgaben helfen, besonders mit Mathe und Biologie. Ich finde sie am schwierigsten. **Jonas**

Wir sind letzte Woche einkaufen gegangen, um eine neue Schuluniform zu kaufen. Mein Vater und ich waren drei Stunden weg. Wir hatten Hunger und sind danach zum Imbiss gegangen, und es hat gut geschmeckt. **Anja**

Ⓗ The verbs highlighted in pink are all irregular in some tenses.
For each of them, write down what tense the verb is in, the infinitive and the meaning.

war – imperfect, sein, to be geblieben – perfect, bleiben, to stay gegangen – perfect, gehen, to go essen – present, essen, to eat bin – present, sein, to be
helfen - infinitive (with a modal verb), helfen, to help
hatten – imperfect, haben, to have (in this context – to be hungry)

\+ Ⓗ For extra practice, write those phrases out and change the word order, putting the time phrase or the **um ... zu ...** / **wenn ...** clause at the start. Think about how this affects the verb.

2. Listen to these four people talking about their free time in 2.1 to 2.4.
Are they talking about things they do now (**N**), in the past (**P**) or in the future (**F**)?

TRACK 36

2.1 N 2.2 P 2.3 F 2.4 N

Was hast du gemacht? *What did you do?*

3. Prepare answers you could say to these questions. Use some of the verbs highlighted on the previous page in your answers, in different persons.

   The questions have been translated to help you.

   3.1 Wohin bist du letztes Wochenende mit deiner Familie gegangen?
   Where did you and your family go last weekend?

   3.2 Was hast du als Kind gemacht? **H** Was machtest du als Kind?
   What did you used to do when you were little?

   3.3 Wohin gehst du nächste Woche mit deinen Freunden aus?
   Where will you go out with your friends next week?

   3.4 Was machst du sonntags zu Hause?
   What do you do at home on Sundays?

4. **H** This student has written **69 words** about a weekend they did not enjoy, in answer to the second bullet point of this Higher writing task. The full task requires **150 words**.
   - your favourite activities to do at home
   - a recent weekend that you did not enjoy.

> Letztes Wochenende hatte ich schlechte Laune. Meine Freunde und ich **sind** in der Stadt einkaufen **gegangen**, aber meine Lieblingsgeschäfte **waren** alle **geschlossen**. Wir **gingen** ins Kino, um den neuen James Bond Film zu sehen, aber er **lief** nicht. Wir **sahen** einen romantischen Film an, aber er **hat** meiner Freundin nicht **gefallen**. Nächstes Wochenende möchte ich lieber in ein Einkaufszentrum gehen, um neue Kleidung zu kaufen. Es **wird** hoffentlich besser **gehen**.

! Notice how, in answering the bullet point, they used two different ways of referring to the past, and two ways of referring to the future. The imperfect and conditional forms are underlined. This increases variety and complexity. Also, there are some verbs in persons of the verb other than 'I' (in bold).

Now it's your turn to have a go at the above task. Write approximately **150 words** and remember to write something about both bullet points.

FREE-TIME ACTIVITIES

Zusammensetzen — *Putting it all together*

1. Read what Michael, Josef and Emilia say about their free time.

Ich male gern in meinem Zimmer, wenn ich zu Hause bin. Kunst ist mein Lieblingsfach. Ich habe letztes Jahr an einem Kunstwettbewerb teilgenommen und habe den ersten Preis gewonnen. Aber ich mag keinen Sport. **Michael**

Ich bin letzten Sommer im See viel schwimmen gegangen. Wassersport und Spazierengehen mache ich am liebsten. Ich bin am Samstag auf eine Party gegangen. Das war schlecht, denn es gab zu viele Personen. **Josef**

Ich liebe alle Sportarten und spiele jedes Wochenende in meiner Schule in einem Team. Ich möchte Spielerin in einer professionellen Mannschaft werden, wenn ich älter bin. Ich möchte beliebt und reich sein. **Emilia**

Match the correct person with each of the following questions. Write **M** for Michael, **J** for Josef or **E** for Emilia.

1.1 Who would like to be famous in the future?

1.2 Who does not like sport?

1.3 Who did not enjoy themselves at the weekend?

1.4 Who won a competition last year?

1.1 E   1.2 M   1.3 J   1.4 M

Photo card

TRACK 37

2. Look at the two photos and make notes about what you can say about them. Then set a timer and talk about the content of the photos.

Foundation **F** students have **one minute** to talk and Higher **H** students have a **minute and a half**. Listen to the recording to hear a student talking about the photos.

Photo 1

Photo 2

Zusammensetzen continued

3. You are writing an article about free time. Write approximately **90 words** in **German**. You must write something about each bullet point.

   Mention:
   - if you prefer team sports or individual sports
   - what you did with your friends last weekend
   - what you will do in your free time after you finish your exams.

Before having a go, take a look at the worked example below, then look back through the whole unit, **2.1 Free-time activities** and write your own answer.

This type of question appears in both Foundation and Higher papers. There is always a bullet point about the present, one about the past and one about the future. Remember to use a variety of verbs (including irregulars and verbs in different persons) and a variety of vocabulary and linking words.

Ich treibe alle Sportarten gern. Ich mache lieber Sport in einem Team, obwohl ich Aktivitäten auch gern allein mache, zum Beispiel Schwimmen. Es ist gut für die Gesundheit. Ich spiele auch gern mit meinen Freunden im Park Basketball, denn wir sind aktiv und es macht viel Spaß, das ist am wichtigsten.

Ich bin letztes Wochenende mit meinen Freunden ins Kino gegangen, um einen Actionfilm zu sehen. Die Kinokarten waren ein bisschen teuer, aber der Film war klasse!

Nach meinen Prüfungen werde ich erst einmal zu Hause bleiben und Musik hören. Danach werde ich eine Party bei mir organisieren. Das wird fantastisch sein!

101 words

obwohl – linking word for two contrasting ideas

zum Beispiel – more complex way of giving an example

denn – introduces a reason for the opinion. Could also use **weil** with different word order

bin ... gegangen, waren, war – good knowledge of perfect and imperfect tenses

am wichtigsten – use of superlative

der Film war klasse! – idiomatic phrase

waren – imperfect tense, third person plural

Nach meinen Prüfungen / Danach – time expressions

werde / wird – in two different persons

2.2

GERMAN FESTIVALS

Besuch bei einem traditionellen Fest — *Visit to a traditional celebration*

1. Read these texts about two German festivals and find the expressions in the texts.

Karneval

Ich habe in den Ferien in Köln den Karneval besucht. Es ist eine alte, historische Tradition aus dem 13. Jahrhundert und ist heutzutage in Deutschland, in Europa und in anderen Teilen der Welt sehr beliebt. Der Karneval in Köln findet im Februar statt. Die zwei wichtigsten Tage sind Rosenmontag und Faschingsdienstag. Man zieht Kostüme und Masken an, tanzt, singt und feiert durch die ganze Stadt. Ich habe mir auch den Karnevalsumzug angeschaut, mit Wagen, riesigen Puppen von Politikern und Gruppen von Clowns und Bands. Die Leute auf den Wagen haben Schokolade und Süßigkeiten auf die Straße geworfen. Die Stimmung war so aufregend!

Weihnachten

Ich habe letztes Jahr mit meinem Freund in Deutschland die Weihnachtszeit gefeiert. Man isst am 24. Dezember (Heiligabend) mit seiner Familie zu Hause ein großes Essen und bekommt Geschenke. Manche Leute gehen danach in die Kirche, um Weihnachtslieder zu singen. Am ersten Weihnachtstag, der ein christlicher Feiertag ist, bleibt man den ganzen Tag zu Hause oder geht spazieren. Jede Familie hat ihre eigenen Traditionen. Das finde ich sehr schön.

1.1 in the holidays
1.2 century
1.3 Rose Monday
1.4 Shrove Tuesday
1.5 costumes and masks
1.6 carnival parade
1.7 the people ... threw
1.8 the atmosphere was
1.9 Christmas time
1.10 Christmas Eve
1.11 Christmas songs
1.12 a Christian holiday
1.13 go for a walk
1.14 their own traditions

der Wagen *wagon, parade float* **die Puppe** *puppet*

1.1 in den Ferien 1.2 Jahrhundert 1.3 Rosenmontag 1.4 Faschingsdienstag 1.5 Kostüme und Masken 1.6 Karnevalsumzug 1.7 die Leute ... haben ... geworfen 1.8 die Stimmung war 1.9 die Weihnachtszeit 1.10 Heiligabend 1.11 Weihnachtslieder 1.12 ein christlicher Feiertag 1.13 geht spazieren 1.14 ihre eigenen Traditionen

Compound nouns

German often puts together combinations of two or more nouns. The gender of these nouns is the same as the gender of their final part.

der Feiertag	*national holiday*
die Silvesterfeier	*New Year's party*
das Weihnachtsgeschenk	*Christmas present*
das Geburtstagskleid	*birthday dress*
das Esszimmer	*dining room*

+ Read back through the texts across these pages and find the compound nouns. When reading any German text, look at the longer words and break them up into individual nouns, and use the contextual clues to help you figure out the meaning of the long word.

2. **H** Fill in the gaps in the text with an appropriate compound noun from the word bank below.

Ich werde am Wochenende ein (2.1) *Stadtfest* besuchen. Es wird mein erstes (2.2) ____________ sein und ich werde draußen sein und das schöne (2.3) ____________ genießen. Ich denke, es gibt an solchen Festen etwas für jede Person. Ich liebe die (2.4) ____________ und das Theater auf diesen Festen. Es gibt eine echte (2.5) ____________ , weil alle zusammen sind. Man hört vielen (2.6) ____________ zu und tanzt, um den (2.7) ____________ zu vergessen und Spaß zu haben.

Partybands Sommerwetter Sommerfest Straßenkünstler Partystimmung Alltagsstress

2.1 Stadtfest 2.2 Sommerfest 2.3 Sommerwetter 2.4 Straßenkünstler 2.5 Partystimmung 2.6 Partybands 2.7 Alltagsstress

Reading aloud

3. Read aloud this passage and then listen to the recording to check your pronunciation.

TRACK 38

Ich finde Feste wunderschön. Viele Leute feiern Weihnachten in Deutschland. Man verbringt Zeit mit Familie und Freunden und bekommt oft tolle Geschenke. Ich gehe auch gern im Sommer zum Straßenfest. Es gibt immer viel Tanz und Musik.

FESTIVALS IN THE GERMAN-SPEAKING WORLD

Wir feiern Ostern — *We are celebrating Easter*

Useful vocabulary

der Schokohase	*chocolate Easter bunny*
die Blume (-n)	*flower*
der Garten	*garden*
das (Oster)ei (-er)	*(Easter) egg*
suchen	*to look for*
der (Oster)baum	*(Easter) tree*
das (Oster)brot	*(Easter) bread*
der (Oster)wein	*(Easter) wine*
(H) entdecken	*to discover*
(H) sich amüsieren	*to amuse oneself*

Describing a photo

Look at the picture below of an Easter egg hunt, and read the discussion prompts.

You could say how many people there are. **Auf dem Foto gibt es drei Kinder.**

You could say where people are. **Die Kinder sind in einem Garten.**

You could say what people are doing in the picture. **Sie suchen Ostereier.**

You could talk about what people are wearing. **Die drei Kinder tragen Pullis und Ohren wie ein Osterhase.**

You could guess what people are feeling and mention your own reaction. **Meiner Meinung nach sind die Kinder sehr glücklich. Ich möchte auch Ostereier suchen.**

You could talk about the physical appearance of the people in the picture, or even the weather. **Die drei Kinder sind klein und ich glaube, das Wetter ist sehr schön.**

1. Now look at the two photos below and make notes on them. Practise saying your answer. If possible, you could record yourself. You need to talk for **one minute (F)** or **one and a half minutes (H)**. Then listen to the example answer.

TRACK 39

Photo 1

Photo 2

Subordinating conjunctions

Some conjunctions (connectives) move the verb to the end of the clause.

bevor	**Man muss ein Kostüm anziehen, bevor man zum Karneval geht.** *You need to put on a costume before you go to the carnival.*
da	**Ich feiere gern Weihnachten, da ich meine Familie besuche.** *I like celebrating Christmas as I visit my family.*
dass	**Ich denke, dass Ostern mein Lieblingsfest ist.** *I think that Easter is my favourite celebration.*
nachdem	**Ich werde das Essen kochen, nachdem ich die Geschenke gekauft habe.** *I am going to cook the food after I have bought the presents.*
obwohl	**Die Kostüme waren fantastisch, obwohl sie sehr billig waren.** *The costumes were fantastic, although they were very cheap.*
weil	**Meine Familie und ich feiern zusammen, weil es lustiger ist.** *My family and I celebrate together because it is more fun.*
wenn	**Ich gehe zum Straßenfest, wenn das Wetter sonnig ist.** *I will go to the street party if the weather is nice.*
(H) damit	**Man tanzt, damit man Spaß haben kann.** *You dance so that you can have fun.*
(H) ob	**Ich weiß noch nicht, ob ich zum Fest gehe.** *I don't know yet whether I am going to the celebration.*

2. (H) Choose the most logical subordinating conjunction for the gap. Then translate the sentence into **English**.

2.1 Ich gehe nicht zum Umzug, ____________ keine Band spielt. (**A** wenn **B** bevor **C** damit)

2.2 Ich glaube, ____________ religiöse Feste wie Eid wichtig für alle sind. (**A** damit **B** weil **C** dass)

2.3 Ich habe Ostern gut gefeiert, ____________ die Musik zu laut war. (**A** ob **B** obwohl **C** damit)

2.4 Ich mag Valentinstag nicht, ____________ ich gar nicht romantisch bin. (**A** obwohl **B** wenn **C** da)

2.1 A I am not going to the parade if there is no band playing.

2.2 C I believe that religious celebrations such as Eid are important for everyone.

2.3 B I had a good Easter celebration, although the music was too loud.

2.4 C I do not like Valentine's Day, as I am not at all romantic.

+ (F) Foundation candidates can still use these sentences. If you don't wish to use the conjunction and change the word order, split the long sentence into two short ones: replace the comma with a full stop and leave out the conjunction. Make sure the verb is always the second idea.

CELEBRATIONS

Was feierst du gern? *What do you like to celebrate?*

1. Read these texts about people's family celebrations. Match the correct person with each of the following questions. Write **S** for Samuel, **M** for Maja, **T** for Theodor, or **L** for Lilly.

Ich mag Hochzeiten! Meine Schwester hatte letzten Sommer ihre Hochzeit. ***Zuerst*** *haben wir viel gegessen und getrunken.* ***Danach*** *haben alle viel getanzt. Ich hatte mit meiner Familie einen wunderschönen Abend!* **Samuel**

Mein Lieblingsfest ist bestimmt Weihnachten. Manche sagen, die Geschenke sind das Beste, aber für mich ist es viel besser, Heiligabend mit der Familie zu verbringen. **Maja**

Ich bekomme zum Geburtstag gern Geschenke von meinen Freunden. Zu meiner Geburtstagsfeier habe ich neue Bücher bekommen, ***und dann*** *haben wir Kuchen gegessen – wie lecker!* **Theodor**

Ich habe eine enge Beziehung zu meinen Großeltern. ***Vor*** *dem Osteressen gehen wir* ***zuerst*** *spazieren.* ***Nach*** *dem Essen gehen wir ins Wohnzimmer und spielen Karten. Um 23 Uhr gehen wir* ***endlich*** *ins Bett.* **Lilly**

1.1 Who likes weddings?
1.2 Who likes going for walks with their family?
1.3 Who likes receiving presents?
1.4 Who spends Christmas Eve with their family?
1.5 Who likes eating birthday cake?
1.6 Who enjoyed a family wedding?

1.1 S 1.2 L 1.3 T 1.4 M 1.5 T 1.6 S

Note the **time markers** and expressions highlighted in bold in the texts. They help organise your ideas and make the text flow more naturally and add complexity. See **page 25** in **Theme 1** for a reminder about time, manner, place.

Modal verbs: dürfen, können, mögen, wollen, müssen, sollen

These very useful verbs are followed by another verb in the infinitive, placed at the end of the sentence. For more on modal verbs and the correct word order, see **pages 152 and 154**.

	dürfen *may, to be allowed to*	können *can, to be able to*	mögen *to like to*	wollen *to want to*	müssen *to have to*	sollen *ought to*
ich	darf	kann	mag	will	muss	soll
du	darfst	kannst	magst	willst	musst	sollst
er/sie/es/man	darf	kann	mag	will	muss	soll

! For **wir** and **sie** (plural) the present tense is the same as the verb's infinitive.

2. Complete the sentences with the correct form of the modal verb given in brackets.
   2.1 Ich ____________ meinen Geburtstag mit Freunden feiern. (dürfen)
   2.2 Ich ____________ noch ein Geschenk für meine Schwester kaufen. (müssen)
   2.3 Mein Bruder ____________ dieses Jahr in unserem Garten Schokoeier suchen. (wollen)
   2.4 Zum Silvester ____________ man Feuerwerke sehen. (können)
   2.5 Touristen in Köln ____________ einmal den Karneval besuchen. (sollen)

2.1 darf 2.2 muss 2.3 will 2.4 kann 2.5 sollen

3. Use modal verbs and vocabulary from the texts on the opposite page to write a sentence in response to each question.
   - Feierst du gern deinen Geburtstag? Warum/Warum nicht? *(Do you like celebrating your birthday? Why/Why not?)*
   - Wie kann man Silvester feiern? *(How can people celebrate New Year's Eve?)*
   - Was willst du zu Weihnachten als Geschenk bekommen? *(What do you want to get as a Christmas present?)*

Practise saying your responses to Exercise 3 out loud. If possible, record yourself and listen back to your recording. These are types of questions which may come up as part of the unprepared conversation that follows the photo card part of the Speaking exam.

CELEBRATIONS IN THE FUTURE

Willst du in der Zukunft heiraten? *In the future, do you want to get married?*

1. Read the interview below about Sabrina's thoughts on weddings and relationships. Select the correct option to complete each sentence.

Ich heiße Sabrina. Meine Familie kommt aus der Türkei, aber ich bin in Wien geboren und wohne hier schon mein ganzes Leben. Ich habe an der Uni Literatur studiert und jetzt arbeite ich in einer Bibliothek.

Willst du in der Zukunft heiraten?

Ja, ich will eine große Hochzeit. Ich will in Österreich heiraten, aber die Hochzeit wird traditionell sein. Ich bin Muslime und für mich persönlich ist es wichtig, einen religiösen Mann zu finden.

Beschreibe deine Hochzeit.

Ich werde ein rotes Kleid tragen mit viel Schmuck. Die Party wird richtig groß sein. Ich werde sicher 300 Gäste einladen. Mein Onkel spielt schöne Instrumente aus der Türkei, also werde ich ihn fragen, ob er für uns spielt.

Wollen deine Freunde auch heiraten?

Einige Freunde kommen auch aus Ländern mit traditionelleren Hochzeitstraditionen oder glauben fest an eine Religion. Sie möchten sicherlich heiraten. Aber eine Ehe ist für manche Freunde aus Österreich und Deutschland nicht so wichtig. Sie wollen lieber eine zivile Partnerschaft.

Möchtest du Kinder?

Ein Paar zu sein, verheiratet zu sein – das ist wunderschön! Ich habe fünf Schwestern und einen Bruder. Ich möchte vielleicht einige Kinder haben. In unserer Familie feiern wir alles zusammen – Geburtstage, Hochzeiten, Jahrestage, Eid. Es wäre schön, diese Momente mit meinen Kindern zu teilen.

1.1 Sabrina and her family are **religious** / **not very traditional** / **Austrian**.

1.2 At her future wedding, Sabrina wants to wear lots of **makeup** / **jewellery** / **dresses**.

1.3 Sabrina wants to ask her **dad** / **uncle** / **brother** to play at her wedding.

1.4 Sabrina's less traditional friends **prefer** / **want** / **do not want** to get married.

1.5 In the future, Sabrina would like to have **two** / **some** / **no** children.

1.6 For her, it is important to **celebrate with** / **teach** / **love** her children.

1.1 religious 1.2 jewellery 1.3 uncle 1.4 do not want 1.5 some 1.6 celebrate with

Negative expressions

In German, negative expressions appear in different parts of the sentence. Usually, they come directly before the thing they are negating.

(gar) nicht	*not (at all)*	Ich möchte gar nicht heiraten.
noch nicht	*not yet*	Ich möchte noch nicht heiraten.
kein	*not a(ny), no...*	Ich möchte in der Zukunft keine Kinder.
niemand	*nobody*	Niemand will jetzt Kinder haben.
nichts	*nothing*	Meine Schwester hat für ihren Geburtstag nichts gemacht.
nie	*never*	Meine Großmutter kocht nie zu Weihnachten.

2. Listen to these four people (2.1–2.4) talking about their plans for a celebration. Are their opinions positive (**P**), negative (**N**), or positive and negative (**P + N**)?

TRACK 40

2.1 P   2.2 N   2.3 P + N   2.4 P

Listen out for key negative expressions to inform your response, if you are unsure about the rest of the vocabulary in each passage.

For practice, listen to the recording again and transcribe (write down) the phrases you hear. Pick out the positive expressions and practise changing them to negative, and vice versa.

Role play

TRACK 41

3. Plan what you are going to say in this role play, taking into account the number of details you will need. Then play the recording, pausing after each question or statement so you can give your response. When you see this **–?–** you will have to ask a question.
   - 3.1 Say what is your favourite festival or celebration. (Give **one** detail.)
   - 3.2 Say what festival you would like to visit in the future.
   - 3.3 Give your opinion on marriage.
   - 3.4 Say whether or not you want children. (Give **two** details.)
   - **?** 3.5 Ask your friend a question about future celebrations.

CELEBRATIONS IN THE PAST

Frohe Weihnachten! *Merry Christmas!*

Useful vocabulary

Heiliger Abend	*Christmas Eve*	**Silvester**	*New Year's Eve*
der erste Weihnachtstag	*Christmas Day*	**das Feuerwerk**	*fireworks*
die Kirche	*church*	**der Spaziergang**	*walk*
das Geschenk	*present*	**der Familienbesuch**	*family visit*
das Weihnachtsessen	*Christmas dinner*	**Frohes Neues Jahr!**	*Happy New Year!*

1. Read the following email in which Nele describes her Christmas celebrations.

Hallo Mika,

wie geht's? Ich bin im Moment in einer Kleinstadt in der Nähe von München. Hier verbringen meine Familie und ich Weihnachten. Normalerweise bleiben wir zu Hause in Hamburg, aber dieses Jahr nicht! Meine Großeltern haben seit drei Jahren ein wunderschönes Haus in Süddeutschland. Es gefällt mir, obwohl das Wetter unglaublich kalt ist. Nächstes Jahr werden wir alle zusammen in Österreich Weihnachten feiern und Ski fahren.

Heute haben wir einen Spaziergang auf dem Land gemacht und viel geredet. Heute Abend ist Heiliger Abend. Wir werden unser Weihnachtsessen genießen und Geschenke bekommen. Danach gehen wir in die Kirche.

Kommst du immer noch zu Silvester zu uns? Wir werden mit meiner Familie ins Restaurant gehen und uns dann das Feuerwerk ansehen. Ich freue mich sehr darauf!

Nele

Write down whether each activity in the list below is happening now (**N**), happened in the past (**P**), or will happen in the future (**F**).

1.1 Spending Christmas at home
1.2 Spending Christmas with the grandparents
1.3 Experiencing cold weather
1.4 Spending Christmas in Austria
1.5 Going for a walk
1.6 Receiving presents
1.7 Going to church
1.8 Watching fireworks for New Year's Eve

1.1 P 1.2 N 1.3 N 1.4 F 1.5 P 1.6 F 1.7 F 1.8 F

Frohe Weihnachten! continued

Dictation

TRACK 42

2. Listen to these five sentences and write them down in **German**. You will hear them once in full, a second time in sections, and once again in full the third time through.

2.1 Ich hatte ein schönes Weihnachten.
2.2 Ich war auf der Silvesterfeier glücklich.
2.3 Gestern Abend war ich zu müde.
2.4 H Wir hatten zu Hause leckeres Essen.
2.5 H Meine Eltern waren dieses Jahr nicht froh.

\+

These imperfect tense forms of **sein** (*to be*) and **haben** (*to have*) are the imperfect tense verbs you will likely see and hear most frequently.

Wie hast du Silvester gefeiert? *How did you celebrate New Year's Eve?*

The last part of your speaking exam is the photo card. You will have to **talk about two photos** for about **one minute** for Foundation or **one and a half minutes** for Higher. After that, you will have an **unprepared conversation** on the theme of the card, for **three to four minutes** for Foundation, or **four and a half to five and a half minutes** for Higher. You will need to demonstrate good variety in your language, vocabulary and tenses, and extend your responses to questions.

3. Translate the following questions into **English**. Then prepare answers for each of them in **German**.

3.1 Was ist dein Lieblingsfest? Warum?
3.2 Feierst du gern deinen Geburtstag? Warum/Warum nicht?
3.3 Was machst du in den Weihnachtsferien mit deiner Familie?
3.4 Wie hast du letztes Jahr deinen Geburtstag gefeiert?
3.5 Welches Fest hast du neulich gefeiert? Wie war es?
3.6 Wo wirst du nächstes Jahr deine Weihnachtsferien verbringen?
3.7 Welches deutsche, Schweizer oder österreichische Fest möchtest du in der Zukunft feiern?
3.8 Willst du in der Zukunft heiraten? Warum/Warum nicht?

3.1 What is your favourite festival? Why?
3.2 Do you like celebrating your birthday? Why/Why not?
3.3 What do you do in the Christmas holidays with your family?
3.4 How did you celebrate your birthday last year?
3.5 What festival did you celebrate recently? How was it?
3.6 Where are you going to spend your Christmas holidays next year?
3.7 Which German, Swiss or Austrian holiday/festival would you like to celebrate in the future?
3.8 Do you want to get married in the future? Why / Why not?

CUSTOMS, FESTIVALS AND CELEBRATIONS

Zusammensetzen — *Putting it all together*

1. Choose the correct option for the gap. This type of exercise appears in the Foundation (F) writing exam only.

1.1 Ich mag zu Silvester die ____________________ Feuerwerke.

wunderschön **wunderschönes** **wunderschönen**

1.2 Man ____________________ zu Karneval auf der Straße singen und tanzen.

sollen **soll** **solltest**

1.3 Mein Bruder ____________________ seinen Geburtstag gern.

feiert **feiern** **feiere**

1.5 Letztes Jahr ____________________ die Osterferien sehr entspannend.

war **sind** **waren**

1.1 wunderschönen *1.2 soll* *1.3 feiert* *1.4 waren*

2. Look at the two photos and make notes about what you can say about them. Then set a timer and talk about the content of the photos.
You need to talk for **one minute** (F) or **one and a half minutes** (H). Then listen to the recording to hear an example of what could be said.

TRACK 43

Photo 1

Photo 2

Zusammensetzen continued

3. Translate the following into **German**.
   - 3.1 I have a birthday party every year.
   - 3.2 Last year, I went to a restaurant to celebrate my birthday.
   - 3.3 I am going to go to a festival next year, because it would be interesting.
   - 3.4 We celebrated my sister's marriage last weekend.
   - 3.5 (H) Lots of people gave me presents yesterday.

3.1 Ich habe jedes Jahr eine Geburtstagsfeier.

3.2 Ich bin letztes Jahr ins Restaurant gegangen, um meinen Geburtstag zu feiern.

3.3 Ich werde nächstes Jahr ein Fest besuchen, denn das wäre interessant. / (H) Nächstes Jahr werde ich ein Fest besuchen, weil das interessant wäre.

3.4 Wir haben letztes Wochenende die Hochzeit meiner Schwester gefeiert.

3.5 Viele Leute haben mir gestern Geschenke gegeben.

4. This student has written **83 words** about a past visit to a festival, in answer to the second bullet point of this (H) Higher writing task. The full task would require **150 words**.

   Mention:
   - how you prefer to celebrate family events
   - a recent visit to a German, Austrian or Swiss festival.

Vor zwei Jahren sind meine Familie und ich nach Köln gefahren, um den Karneval zu besuchen, und es war unglaublich. Viele Leute haben traditionelle Kleidung getragen und ich habe auf den Straßen getanzt. Wir haben einmal deutsche Gerichte gegessen. Die Suppe mit Gemüse und Fisch hat mir sehr geschmeckt, obwohl ich normalerweise Vegetarierin bin. Wenn ich älter bin, möchte ich andere Feste besuchen, weil diese Traditionen mich interessieren. Ich glaube, dass es wichtig ist, an deutschen Festen teilzunehmen und deutsche Kultur zu feiern.

! Note the different tenses – the second bullet point requires an answer in the past, and both the imperfect and perfect have been used to fulfil this. After that, there is a verb in the conditional (**ich möchte**) and a subordinate clause with two infinitives at the end (**teilzunehmen**, **feiern**).

5. (H) You are emailing a friend about holidays. Write approximately **150 words** in **German**. You must write something about both bullet points.

   Mention:
   - how you prefer to celebrate family events
   - a recent visit to a German, Austrian or Swiss festival.

CELEBRITIES

Mein Lieblingsstar — *My favourite celebrity*

Useful vocabulary

bekannt, beliebt, berühmt	*well-known, popular, famous*	der Star die Persönlichkeit	*star, celebrity*
verheiratet	*married*	das Lied	*song*
reich	*rich, wealthy*	die Musikgruppe	*band*
erfolgreich	*successful*	das Publikum	*audience, public*
europäisch	*European*	der/die Sänger/in	*singer*
österreichisch	*Austrian*	der/die Schauspieler/in	*actor*
Schweizer	*Swiss*	die Vorstellung	*performance*

1. Read these two texts about an actor and a singer.
   Do the details below apply to Georg (**G**), Nora (**N**) or both (**G + N**)?

Georg ist ein berühmter österreichischer Schauspieler. Er ist mit einer Schauspielerin verheiratet. Er hat in seiner Karriere viele Preise gewonnen, zum Beispiel einen Oscar. Er arbeitet oft in Österreich und er ist für seine Filme auch in Hollywood bekannt, wo er mit viel Erfolg viele Rollen auf Englisch gespielt hat. Er benutzt keine sozialen Medien.

Nora ist eine Sängerin aus der Schweiz und hat über 17 Millionen Fans. Sie ist in Deutschland geboren und mit ihrem Vater in die Schweiz gekommen, wo sie beliebt ist. Sie arbeitet als Sängerin und Schauspielerin. Sie wohnt auch in der Türkei, wo sie in einer Musikgruppe spielt. Sie hat viele Musikpreise gewonnen und ist international sehr erfolgreich. Sie ist nicht verheiratet und möchte keinen Partner haben.

1.1 is married
1.2 has an international career
1.3 has more than one job
1.4 has won awards
1.5 works internationally
1.6 speaks English
1.7 moved to a different country
1.8 doesn't use social media

1.1 G 1.2 G + N 1.3 N 1.4 G + N 1.5 G + N 1.6 G 1.7 N 1.8 G

! Notice how you can add the **k** in front of the indefinite article **ein/eine** to say 'none of/no'.
Sie gewinnt einen Preis für diese Rolle. She wins a prize for this role.
Sie gewinnt <u>k</u>einen Preis/<u>k</u>eine Preise für diese Rolle. She wins **<u>no</u>** prize(s) for this role.

Mein Lieblingsstar continued

2. Ⓗ Listen to extracts of an interview with Miles, a German YouTuber, and answer the questions in **English**.

TRACK 44

2.1 How did Miles's interest in media start?

2.2 Why did he decide to start on YouTube?

2.3 What advantage of being a YouTuber does Miles mention?

2.4 What are the disadvantages?

2.5 What topics does Miles talk about on his channel?

2.1 He used to write for the school newspaper and then started to write for one of Germany's big newspapers as a journalist.

2.2 He can talk about more varied topics, and he can invite guests onto his show.

2.3 You can be your own boss / decide when and how often you are working.

2.4 He often works weekends and evenings / has little time for his family.

2.5 Current events, fashion and celebrity interviews.

In listening exercises, sometimes you are going to need more than one piece of information to get a mark. If you hear two answers to the question, and they do not contradict each other, write both. Brainstorm a range of possible answers to the questions in English before listening to the passage, to prepare you for what you might hear.

Ⓗ Word order – wo as a subordinating conjunction

Just like the connectors in subordinate clauses on **page 67**, **wo** can be used as a subordinating connector. It moves the verb to the end of the clause after it.

Mein Lieblingsstar kommt aus Wien, wo er als Sänger arbeitet.

My favourite celebrity comes from Vienna, where he works as a singer.

3. Write some sentences about your favourite celebrities, using Exercise 1 as a model to help you. Mention what they do, where they are from, what their following is like and why you and/or others like them. For Ⓗ candidates, try to include at least one subordinating conjunction from **page 67** and remember to check your word order!

   Look at the examples below to help you.

Mein Lieblingsstar ist Lena Stolze. Sie ist Schauspielerin und arbeitet in und kommt aus Berlin. Sie hat viele Followers, denn sie ist sehr beliebt. Ich mag sie, denn sie ist erfolgreich.

Ⓗ Mein Lieblingsstar ist Lena Stolze. Sie kommt aus Berlin, wo sie als Schauspielerin arbeitet. Sie ist sehr beliebt, weil sie viele Followers hat. Ich mag sie, weil sie erfolgreich ist.

PROFILE OF A CELEBRITY

Welchem Star folgst du online? *Which celebrity do you follow online?*

1. Read this interview with Mathias, a German footballer.

Mathias, hast du schon immer Fußball geliebt?

Nein, nicht immer. Ich hatte als Kind in meiner Schule keine Möglichkeit, Fußball zu spielen. Ich habe nur begonnen zu spielen, als ich zwölf Jahre alt war. Ich habe mit meinem Bruder und meinen Freunden gespielt und habe immer gewonnen.

Glaubst du, dass beliebte Persönlichkeiten jetzt mehr Einfluss haben als vor zwanzig Jahren?

Ich denke, beliebte Persönlichkeiten haben jetzt mehr Einfluss als früher. Die neuen Medien helfen viel. Ich habe zum Beispiel ein Interview gemacht und man kann es auf YouTube sehen. Ich hoffe, dass alle, die es anschauen werden, auch Fußballspieler*innen werden möchten.

Interessierst du dich für Mode, wie viele andere Fußballer*innen?

Mode und neue Kleidung sind für mich gar nicht wichtig, denn ich möchte mein Geld lieber für andere Sachen und für meine Familie sparen. Es ist viel besser, wenn ich meine Rolle dazu benutze, anderen zu helfen, und wenn ich Jugendlichen die Chance gebe, am Sport teilzunehmen.

! Gender-neutral forms are common in German publications: you might see an asterisk being used to indicate masculine and feminine forms of words for people.

Find in Mathias's answers in the interview:

1.1 **two** verbs in the imperfect or simple past tense

1.2 **four** verbs in the perfect tense

1.3 **four or more** verbs in the present tense

1.4 **one** verb in the future tense

1.5 **four or more** verbs in the infinitive

1.6 **one** phrase that means 'if I give young people the opportunity'

1.1 hatte, war 1.2 habe ... begonnen, habe ... gespielt, habe ... gewonnen, habe ... gemacht 1.3 (any four of) denke, haben, helfen, kann, hoffe, sind, ist, benutze, gebe 1.4 anschauen werden 1.5 (any four of) spielen, sehen, anschauen, werden, sparen, helfen, teilnehmen 1.6 wenn ich Jugendlichen die Chance gebe

! When you have a text with different tenses, do not assume that each paragraph will include just one time frame. The likelihood is that tenses will be mixed up.

Adjective endings

Remember, the nominative and accusative cases in a sentence mean that a noun is the subject (who/what does the action) or object (the target of that action). This affects which ending to add to adjectives that appear before a noun.

	Masculine	Feminine	Neuter	Plural
nominative (subject)	der reich**e** Star	die beliebt**e** Persönlichkeit	das bekannt**e** Lied	die kreativ**en** Sänger
	ein reich**er** Star	eine beliebt**e** Persönlichkeit	ein bekannt**es** Lied	kreativ**e** Sänger
accusative (object)	de**n** reich**en** Star	die beliebt**e** Persönlichkeit	das bekannt**e** Lied	die kreativ**en** Sänger
	ein**en** reich**en** Star	eine beliebt**e** Persönlichkeit	ein bekannt**es** Lied	kreativ**e** Sänger

! Always learn your nouns with the definite article (**der**/**die**/**das**). There are clues to help you remember a noun's gender. See **page 136** for more information.

2. Your friend saw their favourite celebrity and wrote you a message with these sentences. Choose the correct ending for each adjective, to complete the sentences.
   - 2.1 Ich habe gestern im Restaurant den erfolgreich**en**/**e**/**es** Kinostar gesehen!
   - 2.2 Er hat eine neu**en**/**e**/**es** Jacke und ein blau**en**/**e**/**es** Hemd getragen.
   - 2.3 Er hat ein schön**en**/**e**/**es** Foto mit mir gemacht.
   - 2.4 Meine klein**er**/**e**/**es** Schwester sieht gern seine Komödien an.
   - 2.5 Die überrascht**en**/**e**/**es** Gäste im Restaurant waren sehr froh.

2.1 -en 2.2 -e, -es 2.3 -es 2.4 -e 2.5 -en

3. Choose the correct option for the gap. This type of exercise appears in the Foundation (F) writing exam only.
   - 3.1 Die Person hat gestern ein ____________ Video auf YouTube angesehen.
     lustig **lustiger** **lustiges**
   - 3.2 Meine Schwester hört gern ____________ Lieder.
     deutsche **deutsch** **deutschen**
   - 3.3 Manuel Rubey ist ein ____________ Star in Österreich.
     großer **groß** **großes**
   - 3.4 Ich werde in der Zukunft einen ____________ Film drehen.
     beliebte **beliebt** **beliebten**

3.1 lustiges 3.2 deutsche 3.3 großer 3.4 beliebten

REALITY TV

Die Reality-Shows — *Reality TV programmes*

der Partner/die Partnerin	*partner*
der Wettbewerb	*competition*
die Karriere	*career*
die Runde	*round*
die Wirklichkeit	*reality*
das Glück	*luck, happiness*
das Interview	*interview*

erfolgreich	*successful*
international	*international*
öffentlich	*public*
witzig	*funny*
kennen	*to know*
sich wohlfühlen	*to feel comfortable*
unterstützen	*to support*

Modal verbs in the imperfect or simple past tense

Modal verbs in the imperfect/simple past tense are accompanied by an infinitive at the end of the clause, just as they are in the present tense. You can find the full grammar table on **page 152**.

	ich/er/sie/es/man	
dürfen	durfte	*I was allowed to*
können	konnte	*I was able to, I could*
mögen	mochte	*I liked*

	ich/er/sie/es/man	
wollen	wollte	*I wanted to*
sollen	sollte	*I was supposed to*
müssen	musste	*I had to*

Ich mochte das Interview mit dem Star. *I liked the interview with the celebrity.*
Er durfte keine erfolgreiche Karriere haben. *He was not allowed to have a successful career.*

+ (H) Adding an umlaut to make **dürfte**, **könnte**, **möchte**, **müsste** gives the conditional forms of these four verbs.

1. Translate the following sentences into **English**.
   1.1 Der Star musste ein Interview für die Zeitung geben.
   1.2 Ich wollte gestern meine Lieblingssendung ansehen.
   1.3 Er war alkoholsüchtig, aber seine Familie konnte ihm nicht helfen.
   1.4 Ich sollte nicht fernsehen, wenn ich nach Hause komme.
   1.5 Ich durfte am Wochenende mein Handy nicht benutzen und musste meine Hausaufgaben machen.

1.1 The celebrity had to give an interview for the newspaper.
1.2 I wanted to watch my favourite programme yesterday.
1.3 He was addicted to alcohol, but his family could not help him.
1.4 I wasn't supposed to watch television, when I come home.
1.5 I was not allowed to use my mobile phone at the weekend and had to do my homework.

Die Reality-Shows continued

2. Read these messages found on social media about some reality TV programmes.

A

„Der Bachelor" ist eine schlimme Sendung. Ich finde ihn und die Frauen ganz nervig. Gestern durfte der ledige Mann ein Interview über seine Interessen und Wünsche geben. Das konnte ich nicht ertragen*. Einen Partner im Fernsehen zu finden und dann heiraten – ich glaube, das ist gar nicht romantisch.

B

Programme wie **„Deutschland sucht den Superstar"** machen immer viel Spaß. Man kann sie sich mit der Familie anschauen und über die Lieder diskutieren. Die Sänger und Sängerinnen mussten letztes Wochenende neue Poplieder singen. Mein Lieblingssänger hatte eine wunderbare Stimme, aber die anderen konnten ihre Lieder nicht singen.

C

Ich habe mir die Sendung **„Big Brother"** am Sonntag angesehen und das fand ich sehr unangenehm. Die Personen müssen alle zusammenwohnen und sie streiten sich sehr oft. Es ist für mich zu öffentlich und ich fühle mich dabei nicht wohl.

D

Ich sehe am liebsten **„Ich bin ein Star – Holt mich hier raus!"** Beliebte Stars müssen viele Schwierigkeiten und Herausforderungen* bestehen. Letzte Woche mussten sie ungekochtes Fleisch essen. Wie spannend! Das könnte ich aber nie machen.

Which programme, A, B, C or D, ...

2.1 can you enjoy with your family?

2.2 features some singers who are not very talented?

2.3 puts celebrities in difficult situations?

2.4 features lots of arguments?

2.5 is not very romantic?

2.6 is exciting to watch?

***ertragen** = *to tolerate, put up with* ***Herausforderungen** = *challenges*

2.1 B 2.2 B 2.3 D 2.4 C 2.5 A 2.6 D

Dictation

TRACK 45

3. Listen to these **four** sentences and write them down in German. You will hear them once in full, a second time in sections, and again in full the third time through. (Note that on the Higher H paper there are **five** sentences)

3.1 Die Persönlichkeit ist höflich.

3.2 Ich kenne den Star nicht.

3.3 Der Wettbewerb ist öffentlich.

3.4 Die Sendungen sind immer witzig, aber auch spannend.

CELEBRITIES AS ROLE MODELS

Die Vorbilder — *Role models*

Useful vocabulary

das Vorbild	*role model*	raucht	*smokes*
hilft Leuten, wenn sie Hilfe brauchen	*helps people, when they need help*	trinkt zu viel Alkohol	*drinks too much alcohol*
hilft anderen	*helps others*	verhaltet sich gut/ schlecht	*behaves well/ badly*
ist ein gutes/ schlechtes Vorbild	*is a good/ bad role model*	gibt zu viel für teure Sachen aus	*spends too much on expensive items*
unterstützt Hilfsorganisationen	*supports charities*	ist nicht auf andere stolz	*is not proud of others*

Ⓗ Adjectival nouns after viel, etwas, nichts and alles

Study the examples to see how to use adjectives after **viel**, **etwas**, **nichts** and **alles**. The adjective becomes a noun, with neuter gender and starting with a capital letter. In English, we often translate the phrase with *thing* or *things*.

Er macht für die Stadt viel Wichtiges. *He does lots of important things for the city.*

Es gibt auf YouTube immer etwas Interessantes.
There is always something interesting on YouTube.

Das ist nichts Neues. *That isn't anything new.*

Sie schreibt auf ihrem Blog über alles Gute. *She writes about all the best things on her blog.*

1. Ⓗ Translate the following sentences into **German**.
   1.1 My role model posts lots of interesting things on social media.
   1.2 I like that singer because he always sings about something important.
   1.3 That celebrity has nothing new to say.
   1.4 He has not written anything public.
   1.5 I would like to do something successful.

1.1 Mein Vorbild postet viel Interessantes auf sozialen Medien.
1.2 Ich mag diesen Sänger, denn er singt immer über etwas Wichtiges.
1.3 Dieser Star hat nichts Neues zu sagen.
1.4 Er hat nichts Öffentliches geschrieben.
1.5 Ich möchte etwas Erfolgreiches machen.

Die Vorbilder continued

2. Translate the following sentences into **German**. Use the information on the previous page to help you.
   - 2.1 I like this actor because he helps others.
   - 2.2 Some celebrities have too much money and spend too much on expensive things.
   - 2.3 I watched television yesterday to see my favourite TV programme.
   - 2.4 My parents think they are role models because they support charities.
   - 2.5 The footballer was sad because he drinks too much alcohol.

2.1 Ich mag diesen Schauspieler, denn er hilft anderen.

2.2 Manche Stars haben zu viel Geld und geben zu viel für teure Sachen aus.

2.3 Ich habe gestern ferngesehen, um mir mein Lieblingsprogramm anzuschauen.

2.4 Meine Eltern denken, sie sind Vorbilder, denn sie unterstützen Hilfsorganisationen.

2.5 Der Fußballer war traurig, denn er trinkt zu viel Alkohol.

Role play

TRACK 46

3. Ⓗ Plan what you are going to say in this role play, taking into account the number of details you will need. Then play the recording, pausing after each question or statement so you can give your response. When you see this **–?–** you will have to ask a question. (This is in the style of a Higher tier role play.)
   - 3.1 Say who your favourite celebrity is and what you like about them. (Give **two** details.)
   - 3.2 Say which reality TV programmes you like watching.
   - 3.3 Say how you normally follow celebrities.
   - 3.4 Give your opinion about social media.
   - **?** 3.5 Ask your friend a question about fame.

4. Write about **75 words** describing one celebrity you like and why, and one that you don't like and why. You could say what they do that is positive and negative.

This writing exercise requires you to start your answer in the present tense. However, make sure you show a wide range of language by including verbs in other tenses and persons.

PROS AND CONS OF FAME

Vor- und Nachteile *Advantages and disadvantages*

Useful vocabulary

Vorteile	*Advantages*
Man kann viel Einfluss haben.	*You can have a lot of influence.*
Man verdient viel Geld.	*You earn a lot of money.*
Man kann teure Häuser und Autos kaufen.	*You can buy expensive houses and cars.*
Man hat die Chance, berühmt zu sein.	*It gives you the chance to be famous.*
Man kann interessante Leute kennenlernen.	*You can meet interesting people.*
Man bekommt von anderen und von Firmen Geschenke.	*You receive presents from others and from companies.*

Nachteile	*Disadvantages*
Man hat kein Privatleben.	*You don't have a private life.*
Man hat wenige echte Freunde.	*You have few real friends.*
Man kann nicht für immer berühmt sein.	*You cannot be famous for ever.*
Man muss schön und schlank sein.	*You must be beautiful and slim.*
Leute geben immer ihre Meinung über dein Verhalten.	*Everyone always gives their opinion about your behaviour.*
Alles, was man macht, ist öffentlich.	*Everything you do is public.*

1. Listen to these four people (1.1–1.4) expressing their opinions about fame. Do they express a positive (**P**), negative (**N**) or positive and negative (**P + N**) opinion?

TRACK 47

1.1 Noah: ____________ 1.3 Matteo: ____________

1.2 Emilia: ____________ 1.4 Leni: ____________

2. Listen again. Write in English what reasons they give for their opinions. Write in as much detail as possible.

2.1 Noah: ____________

2.2 Emilia: ____________

2.3 Matteo: ____________

2.4 Leni: ____________

1.1 N 1.2 P + N 1.3 P + N 1.4 P + N

2.1 You may earn a lot of money, but it means nothing because everyone watches everything you do. 2.2 Fame doesn't last forever, but while it lasts, you can meet a lot of interesting people. 2.3 You can buy expensive things, but you don't have a private life. 2.4 Some people are only interested in your money, but you receive a lot of gifts.

3. Read the magazine article about a fashion influencer. Select the correct phrase from the options below to complete each statement.

Charlotte ist auf Instagram als Influencerin bekannt. Für sie spielen Mode, Musik und Arbeit mit Jugendlichen eine große Rolle.

Sie trägt normalerweise moderne, neue, teure Sachen und sieht auf ihren Fotos sehr schön aus. Junge Mädchen schreiben positive Kommentare und möchten wissen, wo sie ihre Kleidung kauft. Charlotte verdient viel Geld und bekommt von Firmen Geschenke.

Sie geht gern auf Musikfestivals, um ihre Lieblingssänger live zu sehen. Viele Leute möchten mit Charlotte ein Foto machen, aber sie findet das manchmal sehr stressig. Ein schlechtes Foto bekommt negative Kritik. Sie hat kein Privatleben, denn alles, was sie macht, ist öffentlich.

In ihrer Freizeit arbeitet sie mit Kindern und sie unterstützt Hilfsorganisationen. Sie lernt oft interessante Leute kennen, aber hat wenig Zeit für Familie oder Freunde.

3.1 For Charlotte, music, fashion and **photography** / **youth work** / **shopping** play a big role.

3.2 Young girls want to find out where Charlotte buys her **gadgets** / **music** / **clothing**.

3.3 As an influencer, Charlotte receives a lot of **gifts** / **criticism** / **messages** from companies.

3.4 Charlotte's life, particularly at music festivals, is at times **thrilling** / **exhausting** / **stressful**.

3.5 Everything Charlotte does is **public** / **private** / **generous**.

3.6 Charlotte spends little time with **family and friends** / **children** / **charity organisations**.

3.1 youth work   3.2 clothing   3.3 gifts   3.4 stressful   3.5 public   3.6 family and friends

4. Read aloud this passage and then listen to the recording to check your pronunciation.

TRACK 48

Es gibt viele positive Seiten, wenn man bekannt ist.

Man wird für junge Leute ein Vorbild und kann anderen helfen.

Aber man ist ab und zu nicht so glücklich.

Man kann sich manchmal allein fühlen.

Freunde und Familie sollten dich unterstützen.

5. Now come up with your own answers to the questions below. Use the vocabulary and phrases from these pages to help you.
   - Was sind die Vor- und Nachteile, wenn man berühmt ist?
   - Möchtest du in der Zukunft berühmt werden? Warum/Warum nicht?

CELEBRITY CULTURE

Zusammensetzen *Putting it all together*

1. Choose the correct option for the gap. This type of exercise appears in the Foundation F writing exam only.

   1.1 Meine Eltern ____________________ nie soziale Medien, um Nachrichten zu schicken.
   benutze **benutzen** **benutzt**

   1.2 Manche Stars sind für junge Leute keine ____________________ Vorbilder.
   guten **gut** **guter**

   1.3 Mein Bruder ____________________ viele Apps auf seinem Handy.
   gehabt **hat** **habe**

   1.5 Man kann im Fernsehen Musik ____________________ .
   hört **hören** **gehört**

1.1 benutzen 1.2 guten 1.3 hat 1.4 hören

2. Listen to a conversation between two Austrian teenagers, Malia and Jannis. Read the sentences below. Who expresses these opinions? Malia (**M**), Jannis (**J**) or both (**M + J**)?

TRACK 49

   2.1 There are more advantages than disadvantages to fame.
   2.2 One positive aspect is that you receive many presents.
   2.3 People criticise celebrities' appearance.
   2.4 People criticise celebrities' clothes.
   2.5 Many celebrities don't care about helping people.
   2.6 Celebrities have lives full of luxury.
   2.7 Celebrities can be positive role models.

2.1 M 2.2 M + J 2.3 M + J 2.4 M 2.5 M 2.6 M + J 2.7 J

3. Look at the two photos and prepare ideas on what to say about them. Remember to say something about both photos and to talk for **one minute** F or **one and a half minutes** H. Then listen to the recording to hear an example of what could be said.

TRACK 50

Photo 1

Photo 2

Zusammensetzen continued

4. Read aloud this passage and then listen to the recording to check your pronunciation.

TRACK 51

Mein Lieblingsstar ist eine deutsche Schauspielerin, die Martine heißt. Es ist wichtig, Kultur in deiner Gegend zu unterstützen. Ich interessiere mich nicht für Persönlichkeiten online, denn ihr Leben ist nicht echt.

5. This student has written **41 words** about celebrity culture in answer to the second bullet point of this writing task. The full task would require **90 words**.

   Mention:
   - the best thing about your favourite celebrity
   - how you followed a celebrity last weekend
   - what you would like to do as a future role model.

   Ich bin letzte Woche im Internet meinem Lieblingsstar auf Instagram gefolgt. Er ist Sänger und hat viele Videos von seinen Konzerten. Er hat auch ein Interview mit einer Zeitung gemacht. Das war interessant und auch sehr persönlich. Ich habe viel gelernt.

   Now it's your turn. You are writing an article about celebrity culture.
   Write approximately **90 words** in **German**.
   You must write something about each bullet point.

   Mention:
   - the best thing about your favourite celebrity
   - how you followed a celebrity last weekend
   - what you would like to do as a future role model.

---

6. **H** Use your ideas from Exercise 5 as a starting point for this Higher writing task.
   You are emailing a friend about celebrities.
   Write approximately **150 words** in **German**.
   You must write something about both bullet points.

   Mention:
   - an advantage and a disadvantage of being a celebrity
   - if you would like to be famous in the future.

Remember to add complexities, such as changed word order, talking about different people, and vocabulary, to gain top marks for the Higher writing tasks.

KEY VOCABULARY

Students are expected to know 1200 items of vocabulary for Foundation tier and a further 500 for Higher tier. This list has some of the key vocabulary for Theme 2, but there are many more words listed in the AQA specification and in an interactive spreadsheet on the AQA website.

fernsehen	*to watch TV*
kaufen	*to buy*
lesen	*to read*
einladen	*to invite*
organisieren	*to organise*
feiern	*to celebrate*
tanzen	*to dance*
aussehen	*to look (appearance)*
kennen	*to know (person, personality)*
tragen	*to wear*
das Publikum	*audience*
der Besucher	*visitor*
die Erfahrung	*experience*
der Kurs	*course*
die Tradition	*tradition*
das Fest	*celebration*
Weihnachten	*Christmas*
Silvester	*New Year*
die Leistung	*achievement*
der Künstler / die Künstlerin	*artist*
süß	*sweet*
schnell	*fast, quick*
bequem	*comfortable*
einfach	*easy*
offen	*open*
traditionell	*traditional*
europäisch	*European*
historisch	*historical*
kulturell	*cultural*
traurig	*sad, upset*
witzig	*funny, witty*
persönlich	*personal*
öffentlich	*public*
musikalisch	*musical*
Schlafzimmer	*bedroom*

EXAMINATION PRACTICE

Popular culture – Reading

These people have written their opinions about free time on their school's web page.

Valentin

Allein Sport treiben ist sehr langweilig. Aber es interessiert mich total, Sport in einer Mannschaft zu spielen, denn man kann mit anderen sprechen. Ich gehe auch oft ins Fitnesszentrum, um fit zu bleiben.

Elena

Ich glaube, man soll am Wochenende Zeit mit der Familie verbringen. Am liebsten koche ich mit meinen Eltern und meinem Bruder. Es macht Spaß und ist viel besser für deine Gesundheit als Fastfood oder im Restaurant essen.

Carlo

Für mich ist wandern sehr entspannend. Man ist draußen und kann die frische Luft und Natur genießen. Meine Familie wandert auch sehr gerne, aber ich wandere lieber allein. Ich hatte als Kind Interesse für Leichtathletik, aber jetzt nicht mehr.

Tilda

Ich gehe fast jeden Tag laufen, um mich gesund zu halten und froh zu bleiben. Mein Lieblingsessen ist trotzdem Schnitzel mit Pommes. Ich weiß, ich sollte meine Ernährung verändern und mehr Obst und Gemüse essen.

Answer the following questions. Write **V** for Valentin, **E** for Elena, **C** for Carlo and **T** for Tilda. Write the correct letter on each line. [8 marks]

01 Who goes to the gym frequently? ____________________

02 Who prefers home cooking? ____________________

03 Who likes team sports? ____________________

04 Who likes to be outdoors? ____________________

05 Who does not have a healthy diet? ____________________

06 Who likes to spend time with family? ____________________

07 Who does not do athletics any more? ____________________

08 Who likes hiking? ____________________

Translate these sentences into **English**. [10 marks]

09 Ich lese in meinem Schlafzimmer.

10 Letzte Woche bin ich schwimmen gegangen.

11 Als Kind bin ich sehr oft mit meinen Eltern ins Kino gegangen.

12 Man sollte für den Karneval ein Kostüm anziehen.

13 Manche Stars posten zu viel auf sozialen Medien.

Popular culture – Listening

01–04 Listen to these four people (01–04) talking about celebrities. What kind of opinion do they have of them? Write **P** for a positive opinion, **N** for a negative opinion, and **P + N** for a positive and negative opinion. [4 marks]

TRACK 52

01 ____________________

02 ____________________

03 ____________________

04 ____________________

Listen to Ida, a footballer, talking about her life. Write **A** if only statement A is correct, **B** if only statement B is correct, and **A + B** if both statements A and B are correct. [5 marks]

TRACK 53

05 Ida plays ... ____________________

A for a German team.

B for a Swiss team.

06 Ida ... ____________________

A likes the atmosphere in the team.

B finds training challenging.

07 Ida says that ... ____________________

A some of her teammates need extra support.

B talent is not enough to make you successful.

08 Ida ... ____________________

A hopes to play for the national team.

B is quite young.

09 Ida's plan for the summer is ... ____________________

A to travel to other countries.

B to play in an international competition.

Dictation

TRACK 54

10 You will now hear **five** short sentences. (Note that, on the Foundation **F** paper, there are only **four** sentences.) Listen carefully and, using your knowledge of German sounds, write down in German exactly what you hear for each sentence.

You will hear each sentence **three** times: the first time as a full sentence, the second time in short sections and the third time again as a full sentence. Use your knowledge of German sounds and grammar to make sure that what you have written makes sense. Check carefully that your spelling is accurate. [10 marks]

Popular culture – Speaking

Role play

Ⓗ Plan what you are going to say in this role play, taking into account the number of details you will need. Remember to use a verb in each response.

Then play the recording, pausing after each question or statement so you can give your response. (Ⓗ This is in the style of a Higher tier role play.)
When you see this **– ? –** you will have to ask a question. [10 marks]

TRACK 55

You are talking to your Swiss friend.

01 Say what you think about team sports. (Give **one** opinion and **one** reason.)

02 Say if you play a musical instrument and why / why not.

03 Say what you did with your friends last weekend. (Give **two** details.)

04 Say what the advantages are of watching a film at home. (Give **two** advantages.)

? 05 Ask your friend a question about watching sports on television.

Photo card

06 Look at the two photos and prepare ideas on what to say about them. Remember to say something about **both** photos and to talk for one minute Ⓕ or one and a half minutes Ⓗ. Then listen to the recording to hear an example of what could be said. [5 marks]

TRACK 56

Photo 1

Photo 2

07 After you have talked about the photos, listen to **ten** questions. Pause after you hear each question and try to answer in as much detail as possible.

This part of the exam should last between **three and four minutes** for Foundation tier Ⓕ, and between **four and a half and five and a half minutes** for Higher tier Ⓗ. [20 marks]

TRACK 57

Popular culture – Writing

01 **F** You decide to send this photo on WhatsApp to a friend in Germany.
What is in this photo? Write **five** sentences in **German**. Foundation only. [10 marks]

02 Translate the following sentences into **German**.
(This is aimed at top **F** to **H** level) [10 marks]

2.1 I am cooking dinner for my parents.

2.2 I played guitar last night for an audience.

2.3 After the festival you can go to the beach.

2.4 I never watch documentaries on TV.

2.5 I think that celebrities should be good role models to young people.

03 **F** + **H** You are writing to your Austrian friend about what you like to do in your free time.
Write approximately **90 words** in **German**.
You must write something about each bullet point.

Mention:

- how you would like to celebrate your birthday next year
- if you prefer to go out with your friends or your family
- something a celebrity did that you did not like. [15 marks]

04 **H** You are writing an article for the school newsletter about how young people live.
Write approximately **150 words** in **German**.
You must write something about each bullet point.

Mention:

- a weekend in the past when you had problems
- a description of a celebrity who gives a good example of young people today. [25 marks]

TOPICS FOR THEME 3

Communication and the world around us

Specification coverage

Topic 1 Travel and tourism, including places of interest

Topic 2 Media and technology

Topic 3 The environment and where people live

Information about the four papers for Foundation F and Higher H tiers:

Paper 1 – Listening

Written exam:
35 minutes F, 45 minutes H
40 marks F, 50 marks H
25% of GCSE

The recording is controlled by the invigilator with built-in repetitions and pauses.

Each exam includes 5 minutes' reading time at the start of the question paper before the listening material is played and 2 minutes at the end of the recording to check your work.

Section A – Listening comprehension questions in English, to be answered in English or non-verbally (F 32 marks, H 40 marks).

Section B – Dictation where students transcribe 4 sentences (F 8 marks) or 5 sentences (H 10 marks).

Paper 2 – Speaking

Non-exam assessment (NEA):
7–9 minutes F or 10–12 minutes H +
15 minutes' supervised preparation time
50 marks, 25% of GCSE

Role play – 10 marks, 1–1.5 minutes. F H

Reading aloud passage and short conversation – 15 marks.
Recommended time 2–2.5 minutes F and 3–3.5 minutes H.
Minimum 35 words F and minimum 50 words H.

Photo card discussion (two photos) – 25 marks.
Photo card discussion time:
4–5 minutes F and 6–7 minutes H.

Paper 3 – Reading

Written exam: 45 minutes F, 1 hour H
50 marks, 25% of GCSE

Section A – Reading comprehension questions in English, to be answered in English or non-verbally (40 marks).

Section B – Translation from German into English, minimum of 35 words F or 50 words H (10 marks).

Paper 4 – Writing

Written exam: 1 hour 10 minutes F,
1 hour 15 minutes H
50 marks, 25% of GCSE

Set of three short writing tasks. F only. 25 marks.

Translation of sentences from English into German, minimum 35 words F, or 50 words H (10 marks).

Produce a piece of writing in response to three compulsory bullet points, approximately 90 words in total. Choose from two questions (15 marks). F H

Open-ended writing task.
Two compulsory bullet points, approximately 150 words in total. Choose from two questions. (25 marks). H only.

TRANSPORTATION

Die Verkehrsmittel — *Means of transport*

der Bus

der Zug / die Bahn

zu Fuß

das Schiff

das Auto

Important verbs

fahren *to go by*
fliegen *to fly*
reisen *to travel*

das Fahrrad

das Flugzeug

die U-Bahn

der Bahnhof

der Flughafen

1. Listen to these four people (1.1–1.4) talking. Each person mentions two types of transport, but which one do they decide to use? Write the answer in **English**.

TRACK 58

1.1 train *1.2 walk / on foot*
1.3 boat *1.4 underground / metro*

It is important to listen to the whole recording for each question before you choose your answer. When two or more options are given, you need to listen for other clues to help you work out which options should be rejected.

Prepositions with the dative case

Prepositions are the useful little words such as **an**, **in**, **mit**, **vor**, before nouns or other words. Many common prepositions in German are followed by a noun in the dative case, which affects the form of their articles (the, a, etc.). A full list of these prepositions can be found on **page 157**.

an *on, at* **in** *in, into* **mit** *with, by* **vor** *in front of*

	Masculine	Feminine	Neuter	Plural
nominative (subject)	der Flughafen	die Straßenbahn	das Flugzeug	die Busse
dative (indirect object)	d<u>em</u> Flughafen	d<u>er</u> Straßenbahn	d<u>em</u> Flugzeug	d<u>en</u> Bussen
	An dem / Am Flughafen gibt es viel zu essen. *At the airport there is lots to eat.*	Ich fahre oft mit der Straßenbahn. *I often travel by tram.*	Ich sitze in dem / im Flugzeug. *I am sitting in the plane.*	Ich warte auf dich vor den Bussen. *I am waiting for you in front of the buses.*

! The dative endings for indefinite articles (**ein**, **eine**, **ein**) follow the same pattern: **einem**, **einer**, **einem**.

2. Translate these sentences into **English**.
   - 2.1 Wir müssen um zwölf Uhr mit dem Bus fahren.
   - 2.2 Am Hauptbahnhof gibt es viele Leute.
   - 2.3 Die Touristen fahren oft mit der U-Bahn in Wien.
   - 2.4 Meine Schwester und ich sitzen auf dem Schiff.
   - 2.5 Meine Familie steht vor dem Auto.

2.1 We have to go / travel by bus at 12 o'clock.
2.2 There are a lot of people at the main / central train station.
2.3 Tourists often travel on the metro / underground in Vienna.
2.4 My sister and I sit / are sitting on the ship.
2.5 My family are standing in front of the car.

3. Read Valentina's description of transport in her town and answer the questions.

Die Mehrheit der Leute fährt **mit** dem Auto **in** meiner Stadt, weil es praktischer und einfacher ist. Man fährt auch **mit** dem Bus, obwohl die Busse nicht oft fahren. Es wäre besser, eine U-Bahn zu haben, um den Verkehr zu vermeiden. Leider gibt es eine U-Bahn nur **in** den Großstädten und nicht bei uns. Wenige Leute fahren Rad, weil es gefährlich ist, aber sie gehen nicht gern zu Fuß – es ist sehr langsam und langweilig! Wenn ich ins Ausland reise, fliege ich normalerweise. Ich liebe es, **im** Flughafen zu sein und **im** Flugzeug zu sitzen. Es ist bequemer, als **mit** dem Schiff zu reisen. Die Tickets sind aber immer ganz teuer!

   - 3.1 Why do most people travel by car?
   - 3.2 What is the problem with buses?
   - 3.3 Why does Valentina want an underground?
   - 3.4 Why do few people ride a bike?
   - 3.5 Why does Valentina like flying?
   - 3.6 What is the issue with travelling by ship?

3.1 It is more practical and easier. 3.2 They don't often come/run. 3.3 To avoid the traffic. 3.4 It is too dangerous. 3.5 Likes being at the airport and sitting in the plane/on the flight / It's more comfortable than the ship/ferry/boat. 3.6 Tickets are expensive.

+ Ⓗ Look closely at the prepositions in bold and the underlined articles. Link this to the pattern explained on the opposite page. Practise recognising the different endings and working out whether the noun is the subject (nominative), direct object (accusative) or indirect object (dative) of the sentence. This will help boost your confidence when applying the articles and endings in your own work.

HOLIDAYS

Was man im Urlaub macht — *What people do on holiday*

Useful vocabulary

mit Freunden ausgehen	*to go out with friends*	schlafen	*to sleep*
die Familie besuchen	*to visit family*	klettern gehen	*to go climbing*
sich entspannen	*to relax*	ins Ausland reisen	*to travel abroad*
einkaufen gehen	*to go shopping*	tauchen	*to dive*
neue Orte entdecken	*to discover new places*	am Strand spielen	*to play on the beach*
im See/im Meer schwimmen	*to swim in the lake/ ocean*	durch die Stadt spazieren gehen	*to go walking through town*

! Each infinitive verb in the list above can be used with a modal verb to say what you can do on holiday (**man kann ...**), or what you ought to (**man soll ...**) or must do (**man muss ...**).

Don't forget to put the infinitive verb at the end of the clause.

Man kann im See schwimmen. *You* (or *People* or *One*) *can swim in the lake.*

Dictation

TRACK 59

1. Listen to these **five** sentences and write them down in **German**. You will hear them once in full, a second time in sections, and again in full the third time through.

1.1 Ich gehe gern mit meiner Schwester aus. *1.2 Ich schlafe im Sommer manchmal zu viel.*
1.3 Man soll in der Schweiz spazieren gehen. *1.4 Ich gehe mit Freunden einkaufen.*
1.5 Man spielt bei gutem Wetter am Strand.

! Careful not to mix up your **ie** [= ee] and **ei** [= eye] sounds in German. There are six examples here.

Role play

TRACK 60

2. Prepare your responses and then listen to the recording, pausing after each question to give your answer. Remember to include a verb in each response.

2.1 Say whether you like spending the holidays at home. (Give **one** reason.)

2.2 Say what you do in good weather. (Give **two** details.)

2.3 Say whether it is better to spend time with family or friends. (Give **two** details.)

2.4 Say what you think about activities you do with friends. (Give **one** detail.)

? 2.5 Ask your friend a question about their holiday activities.

Was man im Urlaub macht continued

3. Read this text about what Fabian and his siblings do during the holidays and select the correct word(s) to complete each sentence.

In den Sommerferien mache ich viele verschiedene Aktivitäten. Ich gehe mit meinen Freunden oder mit meiner Familie spazieren. Ich wohne in der Nähe eines Sees, wo es immer ruhig ist. Manchmal spiele ich mit meinem Bruder Tennis oder ich werfe einen Ball für meinen Hund. Bei gutem Wetter schwimme ich im See, aber bei schlechtem Wetter bleibe ich zu Hause und lese ein Buch. Ich koche auch gern, also muss ich am Wochenende mit dem Bus in die Stadt fahren, um Essen im Supermarkt zu kaufen.

Meine Schwester Aurelia lebt in Griechenland und entdeckt oft neue Orte, weil sie Kunstgeschichte mag. Wenn sie unsere Großeltern an der Küste besucht, macht sie viel Wassersport oder schwimmt im Meer. Meine Schwester kann vier Sprachen sprechen. Deshalb hat sie viele Leute aus anderen Ländern getroffen. Ich möchte sie nächsten Sommer besuchen, damit ich meine Sprachkenntnisse verbessern und auch neue Leute kennenlernen kann.

This text is pitched at Foundation F and Higher H level. The first paragraph is written only in the first-person singular (**ich**), whereas the second is a mixture of the first and third person, and has a wider variety of vocabulary, word order and tenses.

3.1 Fabian goes **for a walk** / **hiking** / **climbing** with his family or friends.

3.2 The lake by his house is always **busy** / **quiet** / **sunny**.

3.3 When the weather is bad, Fabian **plays with his dog** / **reads a book** / **plays tennis**.

3.4 Fabian must travel by **car** / **bus** / **train** to get into town.

3.5 Aurelia likes **history** / **history of art** / **art in new places** in Greece.

3.6 Through **water sports** / **her grandparents** / **speaking languages**, Aurelia has met people.

3.7 Fabian wants to visit Aurelia to **see his family** / **practise sport** / **practise his language**.

3.1 for a walk 3.2 quiet 3.3 reads a book 3.4 bus 3.5 history of art 3.6 speaking languages 3.7 practise his language

Your turn!

4. Write **60–70 words** about what you like to do in the holidays. Use some of the ideas from these two pages to help you. Say something about what you do in the holidays at home and in your local area and/or abroad.

DESCRIBING HOLIDAYS

Die verschiedenen Urlaubsarten — *Different kinds of holiday*

In the grid below, each word can connect to **-urlaub** to make a type of holiday.

Kultur- *cultural*	Berg- / Wander- *mountain / hiking*	Natur- *nature*	-urlaub *holiday*
Ski- *skiing*	Strand- und Sonnen- *beach and sun*	Fahrrad- *cycling*	

! Remember to break up German compound nouns into individual nouns to help you get the overall meaning. You might see nouns such as **Kulturreise** *cultural trip*, **Stadturlaub** *city break* or **Aktivurlaub** *active* or *sports-based holiday*.

Comparing different holidays

For comparisons, add **-er** to the end of an adjective, e.g. **schnell → schneller** *fast / faster*. To say 'less', use **weniger** before an adjective. Add **als** for 'than'. To say two things are equal, i.e. 'as ... as', use **so ... wie** around the adjective.

Ein Skiurlaub ist teurer als ein Natururlaub.	*A skiing holiday is more expensive than a nature holiday.*
Ein Aktivurlaub ist weniger entspannend als ein Strandurlaub.	*A sports-based holiday is less relaxing than a beach holiday.*
Ein Hotelurlaub kann bequemer als ein Campingurlaub sein.	*A hotel holiday can be more comfortable than a camping holiday.*
Ein Kultururlaub ist so interessant wie ein Fahrradurlaub.	*A cultural holiday is as interesting as a cycling holiday.*

! Note these useful irregular forms: **gut → besser → am besten** *good / better / the best*
hoch → höher → am höchsten *high / higher / the highest*

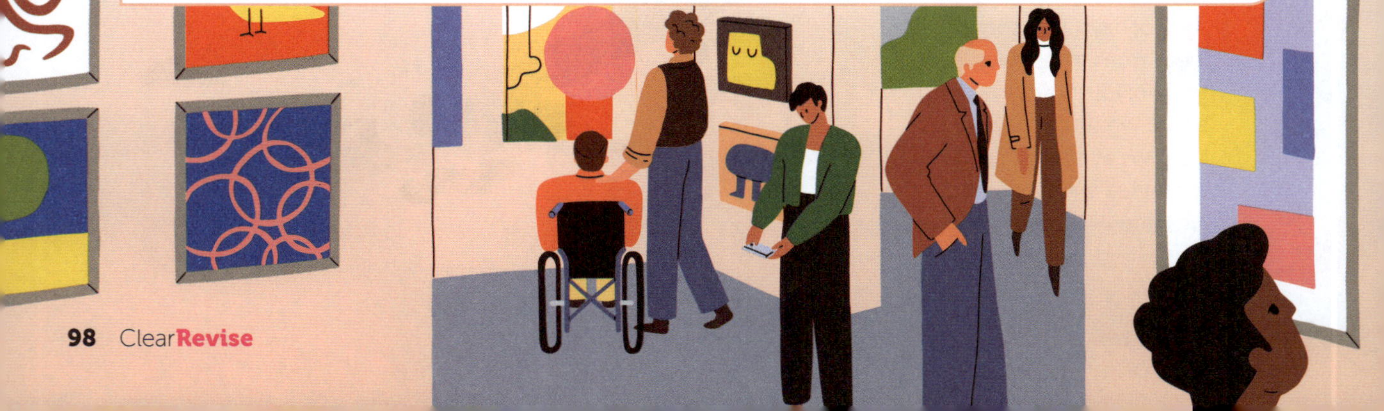

Comparing different holidays continued

1. Match each statement of preference to the most logical reason (A–E).

1.1	Ich finde Strandurlaub besser als Kultururlaub, ...		**A**	*denn ich bin im Grünen und es ist ruhiger als in der Stadt.*
1.2	Ich mache gern Campingurlaub, ...		**B**	*weil ich keinen Wintersport mache.*
1.3	Ins Ausland zu fahren ist interessanter als zu Hause zu bleiben, ...		**C**	*weil man in der Sonne liegen und sich entspannen kann.*
1.4	Ein Skiurlaub ist weniger praktisch als ein Stadturlaub, ...		**D**	*da man neue Orte entdeckt.*
1.5	Am liebsten mache ich Aktivurlaub, ...		**E**	*denn er ist interessanter als Hotelurlaub.*

1.1 C 1.2 A 1.3 D 1.4 B 1.5 E

Giving details about a past holiday

Die positiven Aspekte *The positive aspects*	
Es war sehr warm.	*It was very warm.*
Die Restaurants haben bis spät geöffnet.	*The restaurants were open (until) late.*
Das Zimmer hatte einen Balkon.	*The room had a balcony.*
Das Personal war immer höflich.	*The staff were always friendly.*
Es gab interessante Museen.	*There were interesting museums.*
Ⓗ Wir fuhren zu interessanten Orten.	*We travelled to interesting places.*

Die negativen Aspekte *The negative aspects*	
Wir sind spät angekommen.	*We arrived late.*
Es hat ständig geregnet.	*It rained constantly.*
Ich habe / Wir haben ... verloren.	*I lost / We lost ...*
Es gab ein Problem mit ...	*There was a problem with ...*
Ich war leider die ganze Zeit krank.	*Unfortunately I was ill the whole time.*
Ⓗ Jemand hat ... gestohlen.	*Someone stole ...*

2. This student has written **75 words** in answer to the first two bullet points of this writing task.

You are emailing a friend about holidays. Write approximately **90 words** in **German**. Mention:

- your favourite holiday type and why
- a recent holiday
- where you would like to go on holiday in future.

Ich mache am liebsten Kultururlaub, weil er interessanter und billiger als ein Skiurlaub ist. Man kann neue Orte entdecken und auch Leute aus anderen Ländern treffen. Ich fahre nicht gern Ski, also ist ein Urlaub mit Wintersport nicht praktisch.

Ich bin letzten Sommer mit Freunden mit dem Flugzeug nach Italien geflogen. Es war sehr warm und unser Hotelzimmer hatte einen Balkon. Es gab aber ein Problem mit dem Badezimmer und das Personal war sehr unhöflich.

Write your own answer to the task above. Cover the first two bullet points like the example, or all three for extra practice.

THE WEATHER

Wie ist das Wetter? *What is the weather like?*

Useful vocabulary

Es ist kalt.	*It is cold.*	die Temperatur	*the temperature*
Es ist frisch.	*It is cool.*	Es ist windig.	*It is windy.*
regnen / es regnet	*to rain / it is raining*	schneien / es schneit	*to snow / it is snowing*
Es ist heiß.	*It is hot.*	der Schnee	*snow*
Es ist sonnig.	*It is sunny.*	Es sind zehn Grad.	*It is ten degrees.*
Das Wetter ist gut / schlecht.	*The weather is good / bad.*	Es gibt gutes / schlechtes Wetter.	*It's good / bad weather.*

1. Listen to the weather forecast. Which **two** types of weather are expected in **each** place? Make notes in **English**. (1.1–1.4)

TRACK 61

1.1 Köln/Cologne ______________________

1.2 München/Munich ______________________

1.3 Berlin ______________________

1.4 Hamburg ______________________

1.1 cold, windy   1.2 rain, cool   1.3 sunny, hot   1.4 snow, low temperature

2. Read what these people say about how the weather affected their holiday plans. What was the weather like and what did each person end up doing? Answer in **English**.

Meine Familie und ich wollten im See schwimmen, aber es hat angefangen zu regnen. Deshalb haben wir in einem Café gegessen. **Lionel**

Wir konnten im Wald nicht spazieren gehen, denn es war zu windig. Wir haben auf unserem Campingplatz Lieder gesungen und Musik gespielt. **Nikita**

!

These texts are about past holidays, so they use verbs in the perfect and imperfect tenses: see **pages 149 and 151** for notes on these tenses.

Wir hatten geplant, Fußball am Strand zu spielen, aber es war zu heiß. Also sind wir ins Kino gegangen. **Meryem**

Meine Eltern hatten einen Fahrradurlaub geplant, aber es gab zu viel Schnee. Sie sind zu Hause geblieben. **Alessia**

Lionel – started raining, ate in a café. Nikita – too windy, sang songs and played music at campsite. Meryem – too hot, went to cinema. Alessia – too much snow, stayed at home.

3. (H) Look back at Exercise 2 and adapt the people's texts there, to help you translate these sentences into **German**.
   - 3.1 It started snowing and therefore we stayed in the hotel.
   - 3.2 We stayed at my grandmother's house because it was very cold.
   - 3.3 It was very windy, so we did not go to the beach.
   - 3.4 It was very hot, so my brother went swimming in the lake.
   - 3.5 We went for a walk because the weather was good.

3.1 Es hat angefangen zu schneien und deshalb sind wir im Hotel geblieben.
3.2 Wir sind bei meiner Großmutter geblieben, weil es sehr kalt war.
3.3 Es war sehr windig, also sind wir nicht zum Strand gegangen.
3.4 Es war sehr heiß, also ist mein Bruder im See geschwommen/schwimmen gegangen.
3.5 Wir sind spazieren gegangen, weil das Wetter gut war.

Photo card

TRACK 62

4. Look at the two photos and prepare ideas on what to say about them. Remember to say something about both photos and to talk for one minute (F) or one and a half minutes (H). Listen to the recording to hear a student talking about the photos.

Photo 1

Photo 2

PLACES OF INTEREST

Interessante Orte — *Interesting places*

Places you might visit on holiday

die Insel	*island*	der Wald	*forest*
die Kirche	*church*	das Museum	*museum*
die Moschee	*mosque*	das Schloss	*castle*
der Hafen	*port*	das Stadion	*stadium*
der Markt	*market*	das Theater	*theatre*
der Platz	*square*	die Berge	*mountains*

Adjectives to describe places

alt	*old*	öffentlich	*public*
berühmt	*famous*	ruhig	*quiet, calm*
entspannend	*relaxing*	sauber	*clean*
historisch	*historic*	schmutzig	*dirty*
hübsch	*pretty, lovely*	spannend	*exciting*
kulturell	*cultural*	toll	*great, amazing*
modern	*modern*	traditionell	*traditional*
neu	*new*	wunderbar	*wonderful*

1. Listen to these five people talking about places they visit. Which **two** places does each person mention, and what adjectives do they use to describe them? TRACK 63

   Write notes in **English**.

   1.1 beautiful/lovely castle, quiet forest 1.2 old museum, modern stadium 1.3 historic port, clean island 1.4 wonderful mountains, traditional (Christmas) market 1.5 famous square, exciting theatre

2. Use the vocabulary above and make up **five** different sentences, following these examples and changing the place and adjectives each time.
   - Ich mag **den Hafen**, weil er **modern** und **spannend** ist.
   - Ich liebe **die Berge**, weil sie so **wunderbar** sind.

   Now practise making adjectives agree: place an adjective before each noun, in five more sentences like these examples. (See **pages 140-141** on adjectives.)
   - Ich mag **das alte Museum**, denn es gibt immer **historische Sachen** zu finden.
   - Ich liebe **den traditionellen Markt**, weil es **frisches Obst und Gemüse** gibt.

Direct and indirect object pronouns

These are the main object pronouns you will need. See **page 146** for a complete list.

Direct object pronouns (accusative)	
mich	*me*
dich	*you (singular)*
ihn	*him/it*
sie	*her/it*
es	*it*

Indirect object pronouns (dative)	
mir	*to me*
dir	*to you*
ihm	*to him/it*
ihr	*to her/it*
ihm	*to it*

Das berühmte Schloss hat mich überrascht. *The famous castle surprised me.*
Mein Bruder hat mir zwei Karten gegeben. *My brother gave (to) me two tickets.*

3. Ⓗ Complete the sentences with the correct object pronoun, as indicated in brackets. Then translate the sentences into **English**.

3.1 Ich habe ein neues T-Shirt. Ich habe ________ am Markt gekauft. (*it*)
3.2 Ich habe heute das Schloss besucht und ich habe ________ sehr interessant gefunden. (*it*)
3.3 Ich habe meinen Bruder gesehen und habe ________ die Urlaubfotos gezeigt. (*to him*)
3.4 Wenn du das Stadion sehen möchtest, bringen wir ________ morgen dorthin. (*you*)
3.5 Ich kann ________ den Schlüssel für das Hotelzimmer geben. (*to you*)
3.6 Meine Eltern haben ________ eine Reise mit dem Schiff zur Insel geschenkt. (*to me*)

3.1 es – I have a new T-Shirt. I bought it at the market.
3.2 es – I visited the castle today and I found it very interesting.
3.3 ihm – I visited my brother yesterday and showed him the holiday photos.
3.4 dich – If you want to visit the stadium we will take you there tomorrow.
3.5 dir – I can give you the key for the hotel room.
3.6 mir – My parents got me as a gift/gifted/gave me a boat trip to the island.

Dictation

TRACK 64

4. Listen to these **five** sentences and write them down in German. You will hear them once in full, a second time in sections, and again in full a third time. (Note that on the Foundation Ⓕ paper there are **four** sentences.)

4.1 Die Stimmung am Hafen war spannend.
4.2 Dieser Markt hat eine interessante Geschichte.
4.3 Das Schloss ist ganz alt und sehr schön.
4.4 Mir gefallen die Berge und die Landschaft.
4.5 Viele Touristen finden den Platz zu schmutzig.

TRAVEL AND TOURISM, INCLUDING PLACES OF INTEREST

Zusammensetzen *Putting it all together*

1. This style of question is found on the Reading paper at both tiers. It is called an 'inference' question because you have to infer or deduce what a word means, from the context. These words are not from the defined vocabulary list.

Es gibt überall in Deutschland viele Touristen, in den Städten und auf dem Land. Sie finden es ganz wichtig, die **Sehenswürdigkeiten** wie das Oktoberfest in München, das Schloss Neuschwanstein in Schwangau oder die Museumsinsel in Berlin zu besuchen, um etwas über die deutsche Geschichte und Kultur zu lernen.

What does **Sehenswürdigkeiten** mean?

A festivals **B** historical sites **C** places of interest

The question requires you to read around the word **Sehenswürdigkeiten** and use the clues to help you work out what it means. If you just read up to **wie das Oktoberfest in München**, you might go for option A. If you only looked at **das Schloss** or at **die Museumsinsel**, you might go for option B.

However, if you read further on, it says **um etwas über die deutsche Geschichte und Kultur zu lernen** *to learn something about German history and culture*. This gives you the clue that **Sehenswürdigkeiten** are not just historical, and the meaning is option C, 'places of interest'.

You could also use your knowledge of German compound nouns to break up the word into a verb **sehen** (*to see*) and **würdig** which sounds like 'worthy', thus translating as 'things worth seeing'.

2. Now answer the questions below in the same way.

Letzten Sommer bin in ich mit meiner Familie nach Spanien geflogen. Wir haben für eine Woche in einem Hotel am Strand gewohnt. Eine Nacht gab es ein starkes Gewitter. Das Licht funktionierte nicht und ich konnte in der **Finsternis** mein Handy nicht finden, um die Taschenlampe zu benutzen. In der Stadt konnte ich in den Geschäften auch kein billiges **Andenken** finden, also habe ich für meine Freunde keine Geschenke gekauft.

2.1 **Finsternis** means: **A** light **B** darkness **C** sleep

2.2 **Andenken** means: **A** thoughts **B** memories **C** souvenirs

2.1 B – The text says that in the storm, the light wasn't working and the person couldn't find their phone to use the torch on it. 2.2 C – The person couldn't find any cheap items in the shops, so bought no gifts for their friends. Splitting the word into ***an + denken*** *brings a literal meaning, 'thinking of', so, objects that remind you of a holiday – souvenirs.*

Zusammensetzen continued

Reading aloud

3. Read aloud the following text in **German**.

TRACK 65

> Ich bin gestern mit dem Schiff nach Hamburg gereist. Wir sind um zwei Uhr nachmittags angekommen. Es gab viele Leute, denn man hat das Hafenfest gefeiert. Die Stadt ist bei Touristen sehr beliebt. Ich möchte im Winter die Stadt nochmal besuchen.

Listen to the recording of the passage and check your pronunciation. Repeat any words you think you needed to improve.

4. Complete the following sentences in **German**. Write the correct word in the space.

4.1 Ich fahre lieber mit dem Zug, weil es ____________________ ist.
bequemer **bequemsten** **bequemen**

4.2 Morgen ____________________ es wenige Leute an den Strand geben, da es Montag ist.
werden **wird** **geworden**

4.3 Wir verbringen die Ferien im Ausland, weil es in England oft ____________________ .
Regen **regnet** **geregnet**

4.5 Mit dem Schiff zu reisen ____________________ schlecht, denn es war zu windig.
ist **wird** **war**

4.6 Magst du meine Tasche? Ich habe ____________________ auf dem Markt gekauft.
sie **ihr** **mir**

4.1 bequemer 4.2 wird 4.3 regnet 4.4 war 4.5 sie

Conversation

TRACK 66

5. Listen to the four recorded questions in **German** that relate to travel, tourism and places of interest. Pause after each question to give your response. Try to answer all four questions as fully as you can.

USING A SMARTPHONE

Wie benutzt du dein Handy? *How do you use your mobile?*

Useful verbs

Freunde anrufen	*to call friends*
ansehen/anschauen	*to watch*
bekommen	*to receive*
benutzen	*to use*
herunterladen	*to download*
hochladen	*to upload*
kaufen	*to buy*
lesen	*to read*
Fotos machen	*to take photos*
schicken	*to send*
sprechen	*to talk*
streamen	*to stream*
teilen	*to share*

Useful nouns

die Information	*information*
die Sendung	*programme*
die SMS	*text message*
die Nachricht	*message*
das Handy	*mobile phone*
der/das Blog	*blog*
die sozialen Medien	*social media*
das Spiel	*game*
die Kamera	*camera*
das WLAN	*wi-fi*
die Webseite	*website*
die App	*app*
die E-Mail	*email*

1. Listen to these four young people (1.1–1.4) taking part in a survey about how they use their mobile phone. Which **two** uses does each one mention?

TRACK 67

1.1 sends messages, looks up information online 1.2 takes photos, shares them on social media 1.3 downloads music, calls friends 1.4 plays games, looks for interesting websites

Separable verbs in the present, perfect and future tenses

Some of the verbs listed above have a 'separable prefix' at the front of the **verb**. Its position varies across the tenses – see the underlined part in the examples below.

Infinitive	Present tense	perfect tense	Future tense
anrufen	ich **rufe** Freunde <u>an</u>	ich habe ... <u>ange</u>**rufen**	ich werde ... <u>an</u>**rufen**
(sich) ansehen	ich **sehe** mir Filme <u>an</u>	ich habe mir ... <u>ange</u>**sehen**	ich werde mir ... <u>an</u>**sehen**
aufnehmen	ich **nehme** Videos <u>auf</u>	ich habe ... <u>aufge</u>**nommen**	ich werde ... <u>auf</u>**nehmen**
herunterladen	ich **lade** Musik <u>herunter</u>	ich habe ... <u>herunterge</u>**laden**	ich werde ... <u>herunter</u>**laden**
hochladen	ich **lade** Hausaufgaben <u>hoch</u>	ich habe ... <u>hochge</u>**laden**	ich werde ... <u>hoch</u>**laden**

+ Ⓗ Using these separable verbs in **um ... zu ...** clauses is similar to the perfect tense structure.

Ich benutze mein Handy, um mir Filme anzusehen. *I use my phone to watch films.*

Jugendliche benutzen Handys, um Videos aufzunehmen.

Young people use phones to record videos.

••• *Wie benutzt du dein Handy?* continued

2. Complete the sentences with the correct form of the verb: either the present tense or the infinitive. Then translate the sentences into **English**.

   2.1 Ich ________ sehr oft mit meiner Kamera im Handy Fotos. (machen)

   2.2 Man ________ sein Handy, um Blogs und Nachrichten zu lesen. (benutzen)

   2.3 Es ist praktisch, ein Handy zu haben, denn man kann mit seiner Familie ________ . (sprechen)

   2.4 Ich benutze mein Handy gern, um neue Kleidung online zu ________ . (kaufen)

   2.5 Manchmal ________ ich mir meine Lieblingssendung auf meinem Handy ________ . (ansehen)

---

3. (H) Translate the following sentences into **German**.

   3.1 I use my phone to send messages and to talk to friends.

   3.2 My brother likes to take photos with his phone.

   3.3 Yesterday I used my phone to download music.

   3.4 Yesterday evening I streamed videos on my phone and uploaded my homework.

   3.5 Tomorrow I am going to use my phone to send emails to my family and friends.

2.1 mache – I take photos with my camera on my phone very often.

2.2 benutzt – You use your phone to read blogs and messages.

2.3 sprechen – It is practical to have a phone because you can speak to your family.

2.4 kaufen – I like using my phone to buy new clothes online.

2.5 sehe … an – Sometimes I like to watch my favourite TV programme on my phone.

3.1 Ich benutze mein Handy, um Nachrichten/SMS zu schicken und mit Freunden zu sprechen.

3.2 Mein Bruder macht gern Fotos mit seinem Handy.

3.3 Gestern habe ich mein Handy benutzt, um Musik herunterzuladen.

3.4 Gestern Abend habe ich Videos auf meinem Handy gestreamt und meine Hausaufgaben hochgeladen.

3.5 Morgen werde ich mein Handy benutzen, um E-Mails an meine Familie und Freunde zu schicken.

Your turn!

TRACK 68

4. Listen to the three questions about mobile phones.
   Pause the recording after each one to give your response.

THE INTERNET

Die digitale Welt — *The digital world*

1. (H) Carlotta has written an account of how her family uses the internet. Read what she says.
How do the members of Carlotta's family use the internet?

Ich weiß nicht, wie man früher ohne das Internet gelebt hat! Denn meine Familie und ich benutzen es jeden Tag und für alles! Mein Bruder studiert an der Universität und benutzt das Internet für alle Aufgaben für sein Studium. Er sagt, dass es am nützlichsten ist, wenn man für seine Projekte Informationen schnell finden muss.

Mein Vater geht gern online, um interessante Orte zu finden, die wir im Urlaub besuchen werden. Außerdem kauft er Flug- und Bahntickets für unsere Reise und findet die Hotels, die am billigsten sind.

Meine Mutter arbeitet von zu Hause und benutzt das Internet, um Videoanrufe mit ihren Kollegen zu führen. Sie findet es auch praktisch, Kommentare von anderen Kunden zu lesen, bevor sie einen Tisch in einem Restaurant reserviert. Da sie Vegetarierin ist, liest sie vorher die Speisekarte online, um die besten Gerichte ohne Fleisch zu finden.

Meine Großmutter benutzt das Internet so oft wie uns, um ihre Einkäufe vom Supermarkt zu bestellen.

Write the correct letter or letters.

A	academic research	E	emailing family abroad	I	online shopping
B	booking flights	F	holiday research	J	playing online games
C	buying travel tickets	G	hotel booking	K	reading people's comments
D	checking menu	H	table reservations	L	work video calls

1.1 Brother: ______________________

1.2 Father: ______________________

1.3 Mother: ______________________

1.4 Grandmother: ______________________

1.1 A 1.2 B, C, F, G 1.3 D, H, K, L 1.4 I

+ Superlatives

Superlative forms of adjectives emphasise 'the most', 'the best', 'the greatest'. In German, you use: **am** + adjective + **-sten**.

Ich habe dieses online Video am witzigsten gefunden. *I found this online video the funniest.*

There are three examples in the text above: can you find the German equivalent of these?

the most useful *the cheapest* *the best dishes*

Past, present or future?

A common question on the Listening paper is to identify when an event takes place – in the past, now or in the future (**P**/**N**/**F**).

You need to listen out for the tenses of the verbs, but also listen for time phrases like these:

Past	
gestern	*yesterday*
letzte Woche	*last week*
gestern Abend	*yesterday evening*
vor zwei Tagen	*two days ago*

Now	
heute	*today*
jetzt	*now*
im Moment / momentan	*at the moment*

Future	
morgen	*tomorrow*
diesen Samstag	*this Saturday*
nächsten Sonntag	*next Sunday*

2. Listen to these four people speaking (2.1–2.4) and decide whether the internet activity they talk about is in the past (**P**), now (**N**) or in the future (**F**).

TRACK 69

2.1 N   2.2 P   2.3 F   2.4 P

Sentence building

Read this sentence:

Meine Mutter benutzt das Internet, weil es praktisch ist, (um) eine E-Mail zu schicken.

The ideas in this grid can provide many similar sentences about how people in your (imaginary) family use the internet.

Mein Vater Mein Bruder Mein Onkel Mein Großvater Meine Mutter Meine Schwester Meine Tante Meine Großmutter	benutzt das Internet, weil	es ideal ist, es praktisch ist, es leicht ist, es nützlich ist,	(um) zu lernen. (um) Einkäufe zu machen. (um) Hotelzimmer zu buchen. (um) Tickets zu kaufen. (um) den Urlaub zu organisieren. (um) Videoanrufe zu machen. (um) von zu Hause zu arbeiten. (um) soziale Medien zu nutzen. (um) Musik zu hören.

Your turn!

3. Now use some of the ideas across these two pages to write **at least three ways** in which you and your friends or your family use the internet.
   Try to use sentences in different tenses.

SOCIAL MEDIA

Online Verbindungen | *Online connections*

1. Read these messages found on social media about some reality TV programmes.

Wenn man sagt, dass soziale Medien schlecht für die Gesundheit sind, bin ich mir nicht so sicher. Es gibt nicht genug Informationen darüber. **Alva**

Wenn man sich traurig fühlt, kann man auf sozialen Medien etwas Lustiges finden. Dann geht es einem besser! **Omar**

Es ist super, dass man soziale Medien benutzen kann, um andere Leute kennenzulernen, die sich für die gleichen Sachen interessieren. **Mariella**

Man kann mit Familie und Freunden, die im Ausland wohnen, in Kontakt bleiben. **Damian**

Man sollte soziale Medien dazu nutzen, über etwas Neues zu lesen und anderen Meinungen zuzuhören. **Lene**

Man lernt über Veranstaltungen in seiner Region, wo man wohnt, und man kann Teilnehmer bei wichtigen Aktionen werden. **Frederik**

Which person expresses each of the following opinions about social media networks?

1.1 They cheer you up when you're miserable.

1.2 They're great for keeping in touch with people.

1.3 You get to know people who like the same things as you.

1.4 They make you aware of important causes in your area.

1.5 There is not enough information about the effect of social media on health.

1.6 You learn about different views and opinions.

1.1 Omar 1.2 Damian 1.3 Mariella 1.4 Frederik 1.5 Alva 1.6 Lene

Online Verbindungen continued

2. Translate the following sentences into **English**.

2.1 Ich benutze gern soziale Medien, denn ich kann mit Freunden in Kontakt bleiben.

2.2 Meiner Meinung nach sind soziale Medien nicht so gefährlich.

2.3 Ich habe gestern meine Fotos von meinem Urlaub hochgeladen.

2.4 Ich benutze seit letzter Woche keine sozialen Medien, weil sie mir keinen Spaß mehr machen.

2.1 I like using social media because I can stay in contact with friends.

2.2 In my opinion social media is/are not so dangerous.

2.3 I uploaded photos from my holiday yesterday.

2.4 I have not used social media since last week because it's / they are not fun for me anymore.

3. **H** Listen to these four people (3.1–3.4) talking about the negative side of social networks. Which view does each one express? Select the correct letter.

TRACK 70

3.1 **A** They make you lose sleep.
B People spend too much time on them.
C They make it difficult to have a conversation.

3.2 **A** Some photos can be fake.
B People are on their phone all the time.
C It's all about people showing off.

3.3 **A** They make my life seem boring.
B I spend too much time on them.
C I worry about feeling safe.

3.4 **A** Future employers might get the wrong impression.
B You must be careful about who can see your profile.
C They make you want to change the way you look.

Don't base your answer on recognising one word – it could be misleading. Ensure you listen to the whole recording and choose the answer that best fits.

3.1 B   3.2 A   3.3 A   3.4 C

TECHNOLOGY

Die Nachteile der Technologie — *The disadvantages of technology*

1. Read about people's problems with technology. Find the German for the phrases below.

Papa, ich kann dich nicht hören! Ich glaube, der Ton geht nicht.

Ich muss ein Taxi rufen, aber das Signal ist nicht so stark.

Wie schrecklich! Keine Apps auf meinem neuen Smartphone funktionieren!

Das geht doch nicht! Ich habe meine Hausaufgaben gemacht, aber ich habe alles verloren!

Ich habe einen Videoanruf mit Kollegen, aber meine Kamera funktioniert nicht.

Die Internetverbindung ist so schwach, ich kann nichts online finden!

1.1 I did my homework
1.2 no apps are working
1.3 doesn't work
1.4 the sound isn't working
1.5 the connection is so weak
1.6 the signal is not so strong
1.7 I can't find anything online
1.8 I lost it all

1.1 ich habe meine Hausaufgaben gemacht 1.2 keine Apps ... funktionieren 1.3 funktioniert nicht 1.4 der Ton geht nicht 1.5 die Internetverbindung ist so schwach 1.6 das Signal ist nicht so stark 1.7 ich kann nichts online finden 1.8 ich habe alles verloren

2. **H** Plan what you are going to say in this role play, taking into account the number of details you will need. Then play the recording, pausing after each question or statement so you can give your response.

TRACK 71

(This is in the style of a Higher tier role play.)

2.1 Say how you use your mobile. (Give **two** details.)
2.2 Say how someone in your family uses the internet and why. (Give **one** use and **one** reason.)
2.3 Give your opinion about social networks and a reason. (Give **one** opinion and **one** reason.)
2.4 Give **one** example of a problem you have had with technology.
? 2.5 Ask your friend a question about technology.

Ⓗ Prepositions with dative or accusative

Pairing prepositions with the dative (indirect object) expresses a noun's position or place, whereas the accusative (direct object) with these prepositions indicates movement. A full list can be found on **page 157**. In the examples below, the first sentence expresses position (dative), the second expresses movement (accusative).

an

Dative (expressing position):

Ich sitze an dem Computer / am Computer.
I am sitting at the computer.

Accusative (expressing direction):

Ich schreibe eine SMS an meine Mutter.
I am writing a text to my mother.

auf

Mein Handy liegt auf dem Tisch.
My phone is on the table.

Ich lege mein Handy auf den Tisch. *I am putting my phone on the table.*

neben

Meine Schwester sitzt neben meiner Mutter und redet gar nicht mit ihr. *My sister is sitting next to my mother and isn't talking to her at all.*

Ich lege mein Handy immer neben meinen Laptop. *I always put my phone next to my laptop.*

über

Meine Schwester steht mit ihrem Handy über meinem Bruder. *My sister is standing over my brother with her phone.*

Er hat das Bild über den Schreibtisch gehängt. *He hung the picture above the desk.*

in

Ich sehe mich in dem Foto / im Foto. *I can see myself in the photo.*

Man soll öfter ins Kino gehen, statt Filme zu Hause zu streamen. *You should go to the cinema more often, instead of streaming films at home.*

3. Ⓗ Select the appropriate preposition for each sentence. Then translate each sentence into **English**.

3.1 Ich habe mein Handy auf **den / dem / der** Tisch (*m*) gelegt, aber es ist nicht mehr da.

3.2 Leider habe ich keine Fotos von der Party auf **meiner / meinem / meine** Kamera (*f*).

3.3 Meine Schwester schreibt und postet gern über **ihrem / ihren / ihr** Tag (*m*) online.

3.4 Fremde Leute dürfen auf sozialen Medien nicht an **meine / meinen / mein** Freunde (*pl*) schreiben.

3.5 Der Ton auf **meiner / mein / meinem** Computer (*m*) ist nicht laut, also kann ich keine Musik hören.

3.1 den (acc.) – I put my phone on the table but it's not there / it isn't there anymore.

3.2 meiner (dat.) – Unfortunately I don't have any photos of the party on my camera.

3.3 ihren (acc.) – My sister likes to write and post about her day online.

3.4 meine (acc.) – Strange/Unknown people are not allowed to write to my friends on social media.

3.5 meinem (dat.) – The sound on my computer is not loud, so I can't listen to music.

THE IMPACT OF TECHNOLOGY

Welche Rolle spielt Technologie? *What role does technology play?*

1. **H** These people have posted their views on technology on a forum. Read them and decide whether each opinion is positive (**P**), negative (**N**) or a combination of both (**P + N**).

1.1 ____

Seitdem ich ein Tablet gekauft habe, lese ich viel mehr als früher. Es ist sehr praktisch, da man die **Größe** von dem Text ändern kann. Es ist auch super, wenn man eine **Buchserie** liest. Sobald ich das erste Buch gelesen habe, kann ich das nächste in der Serie kaufen und sofort anfangen.

1.2 ____

Der größte Vorteil der Technologie ist, dass ich fast gar kein Papier mehr benutze. Alles bleibt bei mir im Haus **ordentlich**. Ich schreibe alles auf dem Computer, und ich mache auch etwas Hilfreiches für die Umwelt!

1.3 ____

Manchmal mache ich mir Sorgen, ob die Informationen online echt sind oder nicht. Es gibt einige Menschen, die **gefälschte** Fotos oder falsche Details teilen. Es ist sehr einfach, aber auch gefährlich, an alles zu glauben.

1.4 ____

Wenn meine Freunde diskutieren, ob sie lieber Sport im Park machen sollen oder Videospiele spielen möchten, treffen sie ohne Zweifel die faule Entscheidung! Ohne Technologie wäre es jedoch sehr schwierig, als Team unsere Basketballspiele zu organisieren.

1.5 ____

Natürlich ist es super, dass man im Internet sofort Informationen suchen kann, ohne dass man sich stundenlang an etwas erinnern muss. Aber ich merke schon, wie schnell ich alles vergesse. Ich glaube, die Technologie hat etwas damit zu tun.

1.6 There are **four** words in the texts above, in bold, which do not appear in the vocabulary list. Can you work out what they mean? This is an exam skill you will need to master. Look at the word in context to help you. Break up any longer compound words.

2. **H** Read comments 1.1–1.5 again and find a matching summary for each one below.

A	Is it making me more forgetful?	**E**	It's tempting to just sit and play.
B	I just love my e-reader.	**F**	Can I trust anything I read?
C	It's good for the environment.	**G**	Parental controls are essential.
D	I set myself time limits.	**H**	Online bullying is widespread.

1.1 P 1.2 P 1.3 N 1.4 P + N 1.5 P + N

1.6 Größe – size; Buchserie – book series; ordentlich – organised, tidy; gefälschte – falsified, fake

2. 1.1 B 1.2 C 1.3 F 1.4 E 1.5 A

Ⓗ Adding more complex sequencers

Here are some more complex sequencers and conjunctions (connectives). Use them to challenge yourself and to improve the quality of your written and spoken language.

allerdings	*though, indeed, certainly*
außerdem	*besides, in addition*
bereits	*already*
dagegen	*on the other hand*
damit	*so that, with that*
dazu	*in addition, furthermore*
deswegen	*therefore*

ebenfalls	*likewise, also, as well*
insgesamt	*in all, altogether, in total*
jedenfalls	*in any case, at any rate*
schließlich	*finally, eventually*
sobald	*as soon as*
seitdem	*since, since then*
trotzdem	*nevertheless*

Soziale Medien können ebenfalls gefährlich sein. *Social media can likewise be dangerous.*

Ich schreibe bereits fast nie auf Papier. *I already almost never write on paper.*

Ich denke allerdings, dass ich zu viel Zeit online verbringe. *I do certainly think that I spend too much time online.*

3. Read the short passage. Then rewrite it, adding conjunctions, time phrases and sequencers to link some of the sentences together.

Es gibt bei Technologie viele Vorteile. Man kann Apps benutzen, um eine neue Sprache zu lernen. Man kann sich ein Video anschauen, um eine Antwort auf ein Problem zu finden. Man kann sich auf dem Sofa entspannen und etwas streamen. Man kann Fotos mit Freunden oder auf sozialen Medien teilen. Es ist ärgerlich*, wenn Geräte nicht richtig funktionieren oder kaputt sind. Soziale Medien sind auch als Thema kontrovers. Im Internet hat man alle Verbindungen in der Hand.

* **ärgerlich** = *annoying*

Photo card

4. Look at the two photos and prepare ideas on what to say about them. Remember to say something about both photos and to talk for **one minute (Ⓕ)** or **one and a half minutes (Ⓗ)**. Listen to the recording to hear a student talking about the photos.

TRACK 72

Photo 1

Photo 2

MEDIA AND TECHNOLOGY

Zusammensetzen *Putting it all together*

Reading aloud

TRACK 73

1. Ⓗ Read this passage out loud and then check your pronunciation by listening to the recording of the passage. Then answer the four recorded questions on technology that follow the passage.

Ich benutze mein Handy, um mit Freunden zu sprechen. Ich rufe meine Eltern an, wenn ich spät nach Hause komme. Manchmal spiele ich auch Videospiele auf dem Computer. Morgen muss ich aber anfangen, ein großes Projekt für mein Studium zu schreiben. Dazu soll ich auf verschiedenen Webseiten Informationen finden.

Dictation

TRACK 74

2. Listen to these **five** sentences and write them down in **German**.
You will hear them once in full, a second time in sections, and once again in full the third time through. Note, there are only **four** sentences at Foundation Ⓕ tier.

2.1 Heute organisiere ich unseren Urlaub auf dem Computer.

2.2 Ich habe mein Handy vergessen.

2.3 Ich habe dir per E-Mail meine Adresse geschickt.

2.4 Das Foto ist nicht echt.

2.5 Sie hat keine Nachricht bekommen.

The 90-word writing task

The 90-word writing task that is in both the Foundation Ⓕ and the Higher Ⓗ exam has three bullet points. One requires an answer in the present tense, one refers to something in the past and one refers to the future. It is important to know the tenses well so you can say something in all three time frames.

Here is an example of one of these questions.

3. You are writing an article about technology.

   Write approximately **90 words** in **German**. You must write something about each bullet point.

   Mention:
   - why you think technology is useful
   - a problem you had with technology in the past
   - how you will use technology in the future.

Before having a go, take a look at the worked example below. Then look back through Media and technology, **pages 106–117**, and use the ideas and vocabulary to help you answer the question.

The response below is divided into three sections to clearly show that the three bullet points have been answered. The response is just over 100 words, but it is quality not precise numbers that examiners are looking for.

Worked example

Ich glaube, Technologie ist für unser modernes Leben sehr wichtig, weil es für viele Sachen praktisch ist. Man benutzt das Internet oft, um Hilfe bei seinen Hausaufgaben zu finden, Informationen zu suchen und um Kontakt mit Freunden und Familie zu haben.

Letzte Woche habe ich meine Großmutter mit dem Handy angerufen. Leider war mein Handy kaputt, weil die Apps zu langsam gelaufen sind. Obwohl es ziemlich neu war, musste ich es zurück ins Geschäft bringen.

Morgen werde ich meinen Computer benutzen, da ich Essen bestellen möchte. Ich werde auch Sendungen herunterladen. Ich fahre morgen mit dem Zug und möchte mir etwas ansehen.

um … zu – Uses this to introduce a list of three reasons and create an extended sentence

habe ich … angerufen – Inverts the verb for accurate word order, uses perfect tense of a separable verb

werde ich … benutzen – Uses the future tense

Ich werde auch … herunterladen – Uses a connector and a future tense

weil es für viele Sachen praktisch ist – Gives a reason, and demonstrates knowledge of word order after **weil**

obwohl – Shows good knowledge of word order with subordinating conjunctions

musste ich – imperfect/simple past of a modal verb

WHERE PEOPLE LIVE

Wo ich wohne — *Where I live*

1. Read what Jan has to say about where he used to live and where he lives now.

> Als ich Kind war, habe ich in einer schönen Wohnung im Stadtzentrum gewohnt. Unser neues Haus ist aber auf dem Land. Es gibt zwei Stöcke. Es gibt eine Küche, ein Wohnzimmer und ein Esszimmer. Man geht die Treppen hoch und dann links. Hinter der ersten Tür ist das Badezimmer. Danach gibt es die drei Schlafzimmer und das Büro, wo meine Eltern von zu Hause arbeiten. Es ist ein modernes Gebäude. Jedes Zimmer hat ein Fenster, das Haus bekommt viel Licht und man hat einen Blick auf den Garten. Ich möchte gern ein Schwimmbad! Das haben wir leider nicht, obwohl unser Garten groß genug ist.
>
> **Jan**

Find the German for the following words. Write them in a list with the article (**der**, **die**, **das**) before each one.

floor/storey	kitchen	lounge/living room
dining room	stairs	door
bathroom	bedroom	office
building	window	light
garden	swimming pool	flat

floor/storey – der Stock kitchen – die Küche lounge – das Wohnzimmer
dining room – das Esszimmer stairs – die Treppen door – die Tür
bathroom – das Badezimmer bedroom – das Zimmer/das Schlafzimmer
office – das Büro building – das Gebäude window – das Fenster
light – das Licht garden – der Garten swimming pool – das Schwimmbad
flat – die Wohnung

+ Use the endings on the articles to figure out the gender of the nouns (either the subject or the direct object). Don't worry if you cannot always correctly identify it. It is more important to get the meaning of the noun. See **page 139** for a reminder of endings with definite and indefinite articles across the cases.

Mein Schlafzimmer *My bedroom*

Useful vocabulary

die Pflanze	*plant*	der Stuhl	*chair*
das Bett	*bed*	der Schreibtisch	*desk*
das Fenster	*window*	der Kleiderschrank	*wardrobe*
das Buch	*book*	der Computer	*computer*
die Lampe	*lamp*	das Bücherregal	*bookshelf*

Reading aloud

TRACK 75

2. Read aloud the following text in **German**. This is an example of a detailed answer to the question **Beschreibe dein Haus** (*Describe your house*).

Mein Haus hat sieben Zimmer. Es gibt einen schönen Garten. Es gibt eine kleine Küche und ein bequemes Wohnzimmer. Wir haben drei Schlafzimmer. In meinem Zimmer stehen ein großes Bett und ein moderner Schreibtisch. Auf meinem Schreibtisch gibt es einen Computer und viele Pflanzen. Ich finde mein Zimmer sehr gemütlich.

Listen to the recording of the passage and check your pronunciation. Repeat any words you think you needed to improve.

Your turn!

3. Write **five** sentences about your home. Use a variety of vocabulary to help you practise.

Role play

TRACK 76

4. Ⓗ Plan what you are going to say in this role play, taking into account the number of details you will need. Then play the recording, pausing after each question or statement so you can give your response. (This is in the style of a Higher tier role play.)

4.1 Say what your house is like. (Give **two** details.)

4.2 Say how long you have lived there. (Give **one** detail.)

4.3 Say what you think of your bedroom and why. (Give **one** opinion and **one** reason.)

4.4 Say what your ideal house would be like. (Give **two** details.)

? 4.5 Ask your friend a question about where they live.

TOWNS AND CITIES

In der Stadt *In town*

1. Listen to these five statements about places in town (1.1–1.5). Which **three** things does each person say they have in their town?

TRACK 77

A	bank	**F**	hospital	**K**	restaurant
B	bridge	**G**	library	**L**	school
C	café	**H**	market	**M**	shops
D	cinema	**I**	museum	**N**	stadium
E	factory	**J**	park	**O**	station

1.1 E, C, N 1.2 F, H, M 1.3 L, D, I 1.4 K, B, J 1.5 G, A, O

Talking about where things are

an dem/am an der	*on the, at the (m/nt)* *on the, at the (f)*
in dem/im in der	*in, into the (m/nt)* *in, into the (f)*
in der Nähe von	*close to, near*
von dem/vom von der	*from the (m/nt)* *from the (f)*

hinter	*behind*
mit	*with*
neben	*next to, beside*
vor	*in front of*
zwischen	*between*

+ See how the articles have endings in the dative case, after the prepositions, **hinter**, **neben**, **von**, **vor**, **zwischen**. See **page 157** for a reminder about how this works.

2. Read three people's explanation of how to find the stadium in their city – **Munich**, **Berlin** and **Basel**. Write notes in **English** about where the stadium is.

In München gibt es ein berühmtes Fußballstadion. Es liegt hinter dem Park und vor dem Museum. Die Fußballmannschaft hier ist sehr bekannt. **Josef**

Das Olympiastadion in Berlin muss man einfach besuchen. Um es zu finden, sollte man mit der U-Bahn fahren. Es liegt zwischen der Sportschule und dem Bahnhof. **Katrina**

Man kann das Stadion in Basel sehr einfach finden. Man geht fünf Minuten zu Fuß von dem Park. Es liegt direkt neben dem Einkaufszentrum, hinter dem Café. **Leo**

Munich: behind the park, in front of the museum, Berlin: between the sports school and station, Basel: five minutes from the park, (directly) next to the shopping centre, behind the café.

3. Read the two responses to the question below. Answer the questions in **English**.

Was gibt es in deinem Dorf/in deiner Stadt?

A positive response:

Meine Stadt ist sehr hübsch und bei den Touristen sehr beliebt, weil sie für ihre schönen historischen Gebäude und ihren Markt berühmt ist. Der alte Stadtteil hat viele traditionelle Geschäfte und Restaurants, die gar nicht so teuer sind. Im Stadtzentrum gibt es die Banken und ein Einkaufszentrum. Ich wohne gern in meiner Stadt und möchte in keinem anderen Ort leben. **Alexander**

A negative response:

Mein Dorf ist leider gar nicht interessant, denn es gibt für junge Leute nichts zu tun. Es ist ein altes Gebiet und früher gab es in der Gegend viel Industrie und viele Fabriken. Meiner Meinung nach kann man hier keinen Spaß haben und das Wetter ist immer schlecht! Wenn man ins Kino oder zum Einkaufszentrum gehen möchte, muss man mit dem Bus ins Stadtzentrum fahren. In der Zukunft werde ich irgendwo anders wohnen. **Julia**

3.1 What is Alexander's town famous for? (**Two** details)
3.2 Where can the traditional shops be found?
3.3 What is in the town centre? (**Two** details)
3.4 Why is Julia bored with her village?
3.5 What did the area have in the past? (**Two** details)
3.6 What opinion does she give of her area? (**Two** details)
3.7 In her village, what do they do if they want to go to the cinema?

3.1 beautiful historical buildings and the market 3.2 in the old quarter/district/town
3.3 banks and a shopping centre 3.4 There is nothing to do for young people.
3.5 (a lot of) industry and factories 3.6 You can't have fun and the weather is always bad.
3.7 catch the bus to the town/city centre

To give a full answer to four of these questions, you need to give two details. If you give only one, you will not have provided a full answer and cannot be awarded the full mark for the question.

DESCRIBING THE AREA

In meiner Gegend *In my area*

Look at these phrases you can use to express your preference about where you live.

Ich wohne lieber in der Stadt, denn ...	*I prefer living in the town/city because ...*
es gibt viel zu tun	*there's lots to do*
es gibt überall Leute	*there are people everywhere*
es ist einfach, ins Kino zu gehen	*it is easy to go to the cinema*
die Geschäfte sind in der Nähe	*the shops are close by*
Ⓗ es gibt eine schöne Stimmung	*there is a nice atmosphere*

Ich wohne lieber auf dem Land, denn ...	*I prefer living in the countryside because ...*
es ist sehr ruhig	*it's very peaceful*
die Luft ist sauber	*the air is clean*
das Leben ist langsamer	*life is slower*
es gibt viel mehr Raum	*there is a lot more space*
Ⓗ es gibt weniger Lärm	*there is less noise*

+ If you are writing about the past:

es gibt → es gab *there is/are → there was/were*

es ist → es war *it is → it was*

es hat → es hatte *it has → it had*

mir gefällt / mir gefallen → mir gefiel / mir gefielen *I like → I liked* (sing./plural)

1. Read what some people are posting about their area on the local council website. Do the aspects listed below (1.1–1.6) get positive feedback (**P**), or a negative comment (**N**)?

Es gibt in unserer Stadt leider nicht genug Parkplätze, wo man das Auto parken kann.

Es gab früher viele Touristen, die im Fluss schwimmen gegangen sind. Jetzt ist er aber zu schmutzig.

Ich glaube, die Einwohner lieben ihre Gegend. Man ist schnell in der schönen Landschaft und kann ein interessantes Dorf zu besuchen.

Es gibt immer so viel Verkehr im Stadtzentrum und er ist immer so langsam. Wir brauchen bessere öffentliche Verkehrsmittel.

Mir gefallen die Parks. Vielen Dank, dass Sie noch mehr Bäume gepflanzt haben.

Da es jetzt mehr Busse gibt, ist es viel einfacher, zur Arbeit oder in die Berge zu fahren.

1.1 cleanliness
1.2 green spaces
1.3 parking situation
1.4 surrounding area
1.5 traffic
1.6 transport links

1.1 N 1.2 P 1.3 N 1.4 P 1.5 N 1.6 P

Expressing positive and negative opinions

Look at these ways of expressing the good and the bad about your area.

die Gegend	*area, neighbourhood*
das Gute ist ...	*the good thing is...*
das Beste ist ...	*the best thing is...*
was ich am besten mag, ist/sind ...	*what I like best is/are...*
was mir am besten gefällt, ist/sind ...	*what I like best is/are ...*

das Schlechte ist ...	*the bad thing is...*
das Schlimmste ist ...	*the worst thing is...*
was ich am wenigsten mag, ist/sind ...	*what I like least is/are...*
was mir am wenigsten gefällt, ist/sind ...	*what I like least is/ are ...*

2. **H** Translate these sentences into **German**.
   - 2.1 What I like best in my town are the pretty squares and the parks.
   - 2.2 In my town, the worst thing is the traffic. It is dangerous near the school.
   - 2.3 The good thing in my town is that the transport system is quick.
   - 2.4 I am proud of my area. It has lots of trees and shops.
   - 2.5 What I like least about my area are the streets, as they are often dirty.
3. **H** Imagine you used to live in the city and now live in the country. Write about your impressions of both. Write approximately **150 words** in **German**.

   You must write something about both bullet points. Mention:
   - what you liked and did not like about living in the city
   - what you like and do not like about living in the country.

2.1 Was mir in meiner Stadt am besten gefällt, / Was ich am besten mag, sind die hübschen Plätze und die Parks.

2.2 In meiner Stadt ist das Schlimmste der Verkehr. In der Nähe der Schule ist es gefährlich.

2.3 Das Gute in meiner Stadt ist, dass die Verkehrsmittel schnell sind.

2.4 Ich bin auf meine Gegend stolz. Sie hat viele Bäume und Geschäfte.

2.5 Was mir in meiner Gegend am wenigsten gefällt, / Was ich am wenigsten mag, sind die Straßen, da sie oft schmutzig sind.

3. Example response

Mir gefiel das Leben in der Stadt, weil es viel Spaß gemacht hat und die Stimmung immer gut war. Es war einfach, ins Kino oder zu den Geschäften zu fahren, da alles in der Nähe war. Außerdem waren die Verkehrsmittel sehr schnell. Es gab immer viel zu tun und die Stadt war nie langweilig. Allerdings gab es zu viel Verkehr und ziemlich viel Luftverschmutzung. Es gab nicht genug Platz und überall waren Einwohner und Touristen.

Jetzt wohne ich auf dem Land und mag grüne Bäume und die wunderschöne Landschaft. Das Leben ist langsamer und die Luft ist sauberer. Die Straßen sind nie schmutzig, weil es weniger Menschen gibt. Es ist hier ruhiger und es gibt fast keinen Lärm. Es kann aber auch ein bisschen langweilig sein. Außer Spazieren gehen gibt es nicht viel zu tun und meine Freunde leben noch in der Stadt. Ich glaube, es wäre besser, in der Zukunft wieder im Stadtzentrum zu wohnen. **(155 words)**

THE ENVIRONMENT

Ich bin umweltfreundlich — *I am environmentally friendly*

1. Read this list of advice reminding people what they can do to help the environment. Find the German for the verbs listed below and write the infinitive for each one (ending in **-en**).

1.1 to take ________________

1.2 to let (something) grow ________________

1.3 to separate ________________

1.4 to use ________________

1.5 to plant ________________

1.6 to recycle ________________

1.7 to save ________________

1.8 to reuse ________________

- *Trenne dein Glas, Papier und Plastik.*
- *Recycle alles, was du kannst.*
- *Spare Wasser.*
- *Pflanze Bäume.*
- *Lasse Pflanzen und Gemüse im Garten wachsen.*
- *Verwende dein Plastik wieder.*
- *Benutze öffentliche Verkehrsmittel.*
- *Nimm deinen Müll mit nach Hause! Wir müssen die Straßen sauber halten.*

1.1 nehmen 1.2 wachsen lassen 1.3 trennen 1.4 benutzen 1.5 pflanzen 1.6 recyceln 1.7 sparen 1.8 wiederverwenden

2. Say what you did last week, practising the verbs above. Translate the following short sentences into **German**, using verbs in the perfect tense.

2.1 I planted a tree.

2.2 I saved water.

2.3 I separated the rubbish.

2.4 I recycled bottles.

2.5 I reused a plastic bottle.

2.6 I used public transport.

2.7 I took my rubbish home.

2.1 Ich habe einen Baum gepflanzt.

2.2 Ich habe Wasser gespart.

2.3 Ich habe den Müll getrennt.

2.4 Ich habe Flaschen recycelt.

2.5 Ich habe eine Plastikflasche wiederverwendet.

2.6 Ich habe öffentliche Verkehrsmittel benutzt.

2.7 Ich habe meinen Müll mit nach Hause genommen.

3. Listen to three students talking about environmental projects in their high school (3.1–3.3). TRACK 78

What does each school's project consist of? Write notes in **English**.

3.1 They are going to collect and recycle all the plastic bottles in school.

3.2 They are creating a garden so that they can have fruit and veg in the autumn.

3.3 They had a 'no-car day' and everyone had to walk, cycle or use public transport.

🅗 Giving commands or instructions

When you are telling someone to do something, you use the part of the verb called the **imperative**. This is how it is formed. See **page 153** for more information.

		Example: **fahren** *to travel*
you (informal)	in most cases, take off **-en** ending from the **infinitive verb** and add **-e**	**fahre**
you (formal)	**infinitive verb** followed by **Sie**	**fahren Sie**

!

Note the irregulars:
gib *give*
hilf *help*
nimm *take*
sei / seien Sie *be*

4. 🅗 Translate these sentences into **English**.

4.1 Spare das Regenwasser.
4.2 Hilf der Umwelt.
4.3 Fahre mit dem Bus.
4.4 Benutze dein Fahrrad.
4.5 Trenne den Müll.
4.6 Beschreibe das Problem.

4.1 Save rainwater.
4.2 Help the environment.
4.3 Travel by bus.
4.4 Use your bike.
4.5 Separate the rubbish.
4.6 Describe the problem.

Reading aloud

TRACK 79

5. 🅗 Read this passage aloud and then check your pronunciation by listening to the recording.

Letzte Woche hatten wir in der Stadt einen Tag über die Umwelt. Wir haben den Müll in den Straßen gesammelt. Wir haben kein Auto benutzt. In der Schule haben die Schüler am Schulhof Bäume gepflanzt. Ich habe am Ende des Tages in den Klassenzimmern das Licht ausgemacht.

THE GLOBAL ENVIRONMENT

Globale Themen — *Global issues*

Useful vocabulary

bedeuten	*to mean*
bedrohen, bedroht	*to threaten, threatened*
erweitern	*to expand*
leiden	*to suffer*
überleben	*to survive*
sich verändern	*to change*

verlieren	*to lose*
zerstören	*to destroy*
künftig	*in future*
die Gefahr	*danger*
der Meeresspiegel	*sea level*

1. **H** Read this article about environmental issues and answer the questions below.

Der Klimawandel bedeutet, dass die Welt sich verändert. Das ist nicht nur für Tiere und die Natur ein großes Thema, sondern auch für Menschen. Einige Arten sind jetzt schon bedroht. Wenn wir zum Beispiel eine Art von Insekten verlieren, dann sind die Vögel in Gefahr, weil sie weniger zu fressen haben, um zu überleben. Außerdem leiden Tiere, denn sie haben nicht genug Lebensraum, weil wir ihren Lebensraum zerstören. Wir bauen viel, wo die Wälder stehen, um die Landwirtschaft zu erweitern, ohne über die Folgen auf die Natur zu denken. Man sagt, dass einige Orte in der Welt künftig unter Wasser sein werden, weil die Meeresspiegel ansteigen. Andere Orte werden vielleicht zu heiß, so dass dort keine Menschen mehr leben können.

1.1 According to the article, what **three** things are affected by climate change?

1.2 What could happen if a certain type of insect becomes extinct?

1.3 What else, as well as the climate, is endangering animals?

1.4 What are people doing to create space for agriculture?

1.5 What should they be bearing in mind?

1.6 Why might areas be flooded in the future?

1.7 Why else might certain areas be uninhabitable for humans?

1.1 animals, nature and people

1.2 The birds become endangered because they have less to eat to survive.

1.3 destruction of habitat

1.4 building where the forests are

1.5 the consequences for nature

1.6 rising sea levels

1.7 They will be too hot.

Was kann man tun, um die Umwelt zu schützen?

What can we do, to care for the environment?

Man soll mehr Bäume pflanzen.

Wir müssen die Natur schützen.

Mehr recyceln!

Man muss versuchen, weniger Fleisch zu essen.

Man sollte weniger bis keine neue Kleidung kaufen.

Es ist sicherer, neue Energiequellen zu finden.

Statt zu baden, sollen wir uns duschen, um Wasser zu sparen.

Wir könnten weniger fliegen.

Wir sollten weniger Energie verwenden.

2. Read the recommendations, work out what they mean and find the following expressions:

2.1 we must/we have to
2.2 you/one must try
2.3 you/one ought to
2.4 it is safer
2.5 new energy sources
2.6 you/one should (H)
2.7 we could (H)
2.8 instead of (H)
2.9 little to no (H)

2.1 wir müssen
2.2 man muss versuchen
2.3 man soll
2.4 es ist sicherer
2.5 neue Energiequellen
2.6 man sollte
2.7 wir könnten
2.8 statt
2.9 weniger bis keine

THE ENVIRONMENT AND WHERE PEOPLE LIVE

Zusammensetzen *Putting it all together*

1. Ⓗ Read what Elissa and Raphael say about where they live. Who mentions each aspect listed below? Elissa (**E**), Raphael (**R**) or both Elissa and Raphael (**E + R**)?

Ich wohne in einer Stadt in Süddeutschland. Es ist eine wunderbare Gegend mit Bergen und grüner Landschaft. Es ist eine sehr grüne Region, weil es hier mehr regnet als in anderen Bundesländern.

In den Städten gibt es wegen der Fabriken und Autos Probleme mit Luftverschmutzung. Jedoch ist es einfach, die Stadt zu verlassen und die frische Luft zu genießen. Ich lebe seit sieben Jahren hier und ich denke, es ist der beste Ort der Welt! **Elissa**

Ich lebe in Norddeutschland an der Ostsee. Es ist eine sehr schöne Region mit Städten, traditionellen Häusern und roten Blumen. Allerdings wohne ich direkt am Strand. Es gibt leider sehr hässliche Orte mit riesigen Hotels und Orte, die nur für Touristen gemeint sind. Meiner Meinung nach haben sie das Gebiet zerstört, da es immer zu viele Bauarbeiten gibt. Hier bemerkt man, wie der Klimawandel jedes Jahr deutlicher wird, denn wir kriegen sehr hohe Temperaturen. **Raphael**

1.1 the weather
1.2 air pollution
1.3 the scenery
1.4 traditional homes
1.5 how long they have lived there
1.6 the impact of visitors to the area

1.1 E + R   1.2 E   1.3 E + R   1.4 R   1.5 E   1.6 R

2. You are in Austria visiting your friend, Martin. His mother is showing you around the house. Listen to what she says (2.1–2.4). Select the correct option in each sentence.

TRACK 80

2.1 You will **stay in a university residence** / **share Martin's room** / **have your own room**.
David is **Martin's brother** / **staying with a friend** / **a university lecturer**.

2.2 The bedroom is missing **a cupboard** / **a chair** / **a table**.
The missing item is currently in the **kitchen** / **dining room** / **lounge**.

2.3 The bathroom is **at the end of the corridor** / **next to your room** / **opposite Martin's room**.

2.4 They eat meals **in the dining room** / **on their knees in the lounge** / **at the kitchen table**.

2.1 have your own room / Martin's brother   2.2 a chair / lounge
2.3 next to your room   2.4 in the dining room

Zusammensetzen continued

Photo card

3. Look at the two photos and prepare ideas on what to say about them. Remember to say something both photos and to talk for **one minute** (**F**) or **one and a half minutes** (**H**). Then listen to the recording to hear an example of what could be said.

TRACK 81

Photo 1

Photo 2

4. **H** Translate these sentences into **German**.
   - 4.1 My favourite room in the house is my bedroom, because it is comfortable and peaceful.
   - 4.2 There was a library behind the shopping centre, but they closed it.
   - 4.3 In my town the best thing is that there is a lot to do for young people.
   - 4.4 We collected litter in the school yard, and I helped to plant some trees.
   - 4.5 We must protect the forest and our threatened animal species.

4.1 Mein Lieblingszimmer ist mein eigenes Zimmer, weil es bequem und ruhig ist.

4.2 Es gab eine Bibliothek hinter dem Einkaufzentrum, aber man hat sie geschlossen.

4.3 In meiner Stadt ist das Beste, dass es viel für junge Leute zu tun gibt.

4.4 Wir haben auf dem Schulhof Müll gesammelt und ich habe geholfen, Bäume zu pflanzen.

4.5 Wir müssen den Wald und unsere bedrohten Tierarten schützen.

KEY VOCABULARY

Students are expected to know 1200 items of vocabulary for Foundation tier and a further 500 for Higher tier. This list has some of the key vocabulary for Theme 3, but there are many more words listed in the AQA specification and in an interactive spreadsheet on the AQA website.

besuchen	*to visit*
fliegen	*to fly*
träumen	*to dream*
übersetzen	*to translate*
anrufen	*to call*
benutzen	*to use*
funktionieren	*to function*
schicken	*to send*
bauen	*to build*
organisieren	*to organise*
steigen	*to climb, rise*
verkaufen	*to sell*
die Umwelt	*environment*
der Flughafen	*airport*
der Verkehr	*traffic, transport*
der Blick	*view*
die Insel	*island*
die Sicherheit	*safety*
das System	*system*
das Gerät	*gadget, device*
der Ton	*sound*
das Bundesland	*German federal state*
die Bundesregierung	*German / Austrian government*
die Ostsee	*Baltic Sea*
der Rhein	*Rhine*
die Landschaft	*landscape*
die Luftverschmutzung	*air pollution*
eng	*narrow*
schmutzig	*dirty*
leicht	*easy, light*
gefährlich	*dangerous*
entspannend	*relaxing*
fremd	*strange, foreign*

EXAMINATION PRACTICE

Communication and the world around us – Reading

These people have written comments on their town's web page.

01 Samuel

Weil man das Zentrum verbessert hat und da viele Straßen jetzt autofrei sind, denke ich, dass die Stadt jetzt ein guter Ort zum Leben ist.

02 Romy

Die grünen Viertel sind gut. Einige Straßen in der Stadtmitte sind aber leider noch sehr schmutzig und es gibt noch viel zu tun, um sie zu verbessern.

03 Mika

Meiner Meinung nach gibt es in dieser Stadt nur sehr wenige Aktivitäten für junge Leute. Außerdem habe ich Angst, wenn ich alleine nach Hause gehe, weil es keine Straßenlampen gibt.

04 Nele

Die Wahrheit ist, dass ich mit meiner Familie als Kind viel gereist bin. Jetzt bin ich erwachsen und ich möchte in der Stadt wohnen, wo ich geboren bin. Hier fühle ich mich zu Hause.

What do they think about the town? Write **P** for a positive opinion, **N** for a negative opinion, **P + N** for a positive and negative opinion. [4 marks]

01 Samuel: __________ 02 Romy: __________ 03 Mika: __________ 04 Nele: __________

(H) You read this article about ideas for four different types of holidays.

Wenn man als Familie Camping macht, ist das eine gute Gelegenheit, etwas zusammen zu tun und als Team zu arbeiten.

Man kann auch eine Woche in einem Haus auf dem Land verbringen. Man kommt mit der Natur in Kontakt und vergisst die Probleme, die das Stadtleben oft mit sich bringt.

Wenn man einen Freiwilligenurlaub macht, kann man helfen, ein neues Schulklassenzimmer im Dorf zu bauen oder an einem Umweltprojekt teilzunehmen. Die Projektteilnehmer werden Freunde – und einige werden später vielleicht heiraten!

Ich würde sagen, wenn man Wintersport mag, dann ist ein Besuch im Winter eine gute Idee. Leider ist es in dieser Jahreszeit teurer, in einem Hotel zu bleiben, da es viel mehr Gäste gibt.

Answer the following questions in **English**.

05 What are the benefits of camping as a family? (Give **two** details.) [2 marks]

06 What can a holiday in the country help you to do? (Give **two** details.) [2 marks]

07 What **two** types of voluntary work are mentioned? [2 marks]

08 What do we learn about some of the volunteers? [1 mark]

09 What activity do visitors do in the winter? [1 mark]

10 What negative aspect of winter visits is mentioned? [1 mark]

Communication and the world around us – Listening

01–04 Ⓗ You hear four people calling a radio phone-in programme about new technology. What are their opinions? Write **P** for a positive opinion, **N** for a negative opinion and **P + N** for a positive and negative opinion. [4 marks]

TRACK 82

01 ______________________

02 ______________________

03 ______________________

04 ______________________

Linus is phoning his grandfather to tell him about his week. He mentions two activities. Write the correct number for each activity. Write the correct letter for when it takes place. [4 marks]

TRACK 83

Activity	
1	Revising
2	Sunbathing
3	Watching a film
4	Working

When	
P	Past
N	Now
F	Future

05 Activity: ______________________ When: ______________________

06 Activity: ______________________ When: ______________________

Dictation

07 You will now hear **five** short sentences.

TRACK 84

Listen carefully and, using your knowledge of German sounds, write down in **German** exactly what you hear for each sentence.

You will hear each sentence **three** times: the first time as a full sentence, the second time in short sections and the third time again as a full sentence.

Use your knowledge of German sounds and grammar to make sure that what you have written makes sense. Check carefully that your spelling is accurate.

(Note that, on the Foundation Ⓕ paper, there are only four sentences.) [10 marks]

Communication and the world around us – Speaking

Role play

(H) Plan what you are going to say in this role play, taking into account the number of details you will need. Remember to use a verb in each response.

TRACK 85

Then play the recording, pausing after each question or statement so you can give your response.
((H) This is in the style of a Higher tier role play.)
When you see this **– ? –** you will have to ask a question. [10 marks]

01 You are talking to your Swiss friend.

01.1 Say where you are going to go on holiday and why. (Give **one** place and **one** reason.)

01.2 Say how you used technology to plan your holiday. (Give **one** detail.)

01.3 Say how you like to travel and why. (Give **one** method of transport and **one** reason.)

01.4 Say what you do with friends during the summer holidays. (Give **two** details.)

? 01.5 Ask your friend about the place where they live.

---

02 (H) Read aloud the following passage and then answer the questions in the recording.

TRACK 86

> Wenn ich mit meiner Familie im Urlaub bin, haben wir viel Spaß miteinander. Wir machen viele verschiedene Aktivitäten. Es ist super, da meine Eltern für alles bezahlen! Jedes Jahr kaufe ich Geschenke für meine Freunde. Ich rufe sie auch manchmal an, um zu erfahren, wie sie die Zeit verbringen. Nächsten Sommer wäre es schön, mit ihnen eine Reise zu machen.

This is a Higher tier task. [5+10 marks]

Photo card

TRACK 87

03 Look at the two photos and prepare ideas on what to say about them. Remember to say something about **both** photos and to talk for one minute (F) or one and a half minutes (H).

[5 marks]

Photo 1

Photo 2

04 Now answer the recorded questions for the unprepared conversation on the theme.
[20 marks]

TRACK 88

Communication and the world around us – Writing

01 Translate the following sentences into **German**. [10 marks]

(This is aimed at top F to H level.)

01.1 I used the computer to buy the tickets.

01.2 Lilian helps her grandfather to do his shopping online.

01.3 He did his homework on his laptop.

01.4 Young people spend too much time on their mobile phones.

01.5 I forgot to upload the photos.

---

02 F + H You are writing an article about home and travel.
Write approximately **90 words** in **German**.
You must write something about each bullet point.

Mention:

- what you think about the area where you live
- what you did during the last holidays
- where you would most like to travel. [15 marks]

---

03 H You are writing a post for a website about the environment.
Write approximately **150 words** in **German**.
You must write something about each bullet point.

Mention:

- why you are concerned about environmental problems
- what you are going to do in your school to help the environment. [25 marks]

GRAMMAR

The grammar requirements for GCSE are set out in two tiers: Foundation and Higher.

Students are required to use their knowledge of grammar from the specified lists, appropriate to the relevant tier of entry.

Students completing Higher tier assessments will be required to apply all grammar listed for Foundation tier in addition to the grammar listed for Ⓗ Higher tier.

NOUNS AND ARTICLES

Nouns

Nouns are words used to name a person, place or thing (including abstract ideas). Examples: 'teacher', 'house', 'name'. It often helps to ask yourself if a word can have 'the' before it. If it can, it is a noun ('the teacher', 'the house', 'the name').

German nouns all have a gender: they are masculine, feminine or neuter. Remember that objects or things are not all neuter in German, so you can't always use **es** when you want to say 'it'.

All German nouns begin with a capital letter.

Masculine nouns

Most nouns ending in -**er** are masculine:
Vater *father*, **Computer** *computer*, **Fehler** *mistake*.

Days, months and seasons are masculine:
Sonntag *Sunday*, **Sommer** *summer*, **Juli** *July*.

Words for people

Job titles or roles ending in -**er** or -**ist** are masculine and can be changed to feminine by adding -**in**.

Lehrer → Lehrerin
Betreuer → Betreuerin
Journalist → Journalistin

Feminine nouns

Nouns with these endings are generally feminine:

-e:	**Schule** *school*, **Stunde** *hour / lesson*
-ei:	**Polizei** *police*, **Türkei** *Turkey*
-heit:	**Vergangenheit** *past*
-ie:	**Komödie** *comedy*, **Linie** *line / route*
-ik:	**Mathematik** *maths*, **Musik** *music*
-keit:	**Persönlichkeit** *personality*, **Möglichkeit** *possibility*
-schaft:	**Landschaft** *landscape*, **Mannschaft** *team*
-tät:	**Aktivität** *activity*, **Universität** *university*
-tion:	**Aktion** *campaign*, **Information** *information*
-ung:	**Kleidung** *clothing*, **Zeitung** *newspaper*

Neuter nouns

Nouns with these endings are generally neuter:

-chen:	**Hähnchen** *chicken*, **Mädchen** *child*
-ma:	**Thema** *theme*, **Klima** *climate*, **Drama** *drama*
-tel:	**Hotel** *hotel*, **Mittel** *means*, **Viertel** *quarter / district*
-um:	**Museum** *museum*, **Publikum** *audience*, **Zentrum** *centre*

Using the infinitive as a noun

In English we use the '-ing' part of the verb as a noun, for example: 'Smoking is bad for your health'. In German, the infinitive is used instead, and is treated as a neuter noun: **Das Rauchen ist schlecht für die Gesundheit**.

Plurals of nouns

Most masculine nouns add -**e** or an umlaut and -**e** to make the plural.
Sohn → Söhne *sons* **Stuhl → Stühle** *chairs* **Tisch → Tische** *tables*

Most neuter nouns add -**er**, and an umlaut on the vowels a, o, u.
Blatt → Blätter *sheets / leaves* **Buch → Bücher** *books* **Haus → Häuser** *houses*

If a masculine noun ends in -**er**, there is no additional ending to make the plural.
Besucher *visitor / visitors* **Partner** *partner / partners* **Verkäufer** *salesperson / salespeople*
Notable exceptions: **Bruder → Brüder** *brothers* **Vater → Väter** *fathers*

Most feminine nouns add -**n** or -**en** to make the plural.
Aktivität → Aktivitäten *activities* **Katze → Katzen** *cats* **Schwester → Schwestern** *sisters*

Feminine occupation nouns ending in -**in** add -**nen** to make the plural.
Chefin → Chefinnen *female bosses* **Studentin → Studentinnen** *female students*

Nouns borrowed from other languages usually add -**s** to make the plural.
Auto → Autos *cars* **Band → Bands** *bands* **Hotel → Hotels** *hotels*

Compound nouns

German often puts together combinations of two or more nouns to make longer words.
The gender of these nouns is the gender of their final part.

der Weihnachtstag *Christmas Day* **die Bundesrepublik** *Federal Republic* **die Speisekarte** *menu*

Articles

There are two types of articles, definite and indefinite. In English, the definite article is 'the', and the indefinite articles are 'a', 'an' and 'some'.

In German, there are different forms depending on the gender and number of the noun. They also change according to whether the noun is the subject (nominative case), direct object (accusative case) or indirect object (dative case) of the sentence: see **page 139** for cases.

	Definite articles *the*		Indefinite articles *a*	
	Singular	Plural	Singular	Plural *(no article required)*
Masculine	**der Mann** *the man*	**die Männer** *the men*	**ein Mann** *a man*	**Männer** *men*
Feminine	**die Frau** *the woman*	**die Frauen** *the women*	**eine Frau** *a woman*	**Frauen** *women*
Neuter	**das Kind** *the child*	**die Kinder** *the children*	**ein Kind** *a child*	**Kinder** *children*

! Unlike in English, the definite article can be used in German to indicate when you are generalising: **Die Kultur ist wichtig.** *Culture is important.*

The indefinite article in German is omitted after **sein** when followed by an occupation or profession: **Mein Vater ist Lehrer.** *My father is a teacher.*

CASES

In an English sentence like 'The dog is eating the apple!' the two definite articles are the same – 'the'. In German, the articles are different, depending on grammatical cases; so that sentence would need der and den: Der Hund isst den Apfel!

The endings of articles and adjectives in a sentence relate to who or what does the action (the subject), and who or what is the target or object of that action.

German has four cases in total: nominative (the subject of the sentence); accusative (the direct object); dative (the indirect object); and genitive (illustrating a relationship between two nouns).

! The genitive case is the least common of the four cases. Candidates at Foundation Ⓕ and Higher Ⓗ tier need to know the nominative, accusative and dative cases. Only candidates at Higher Ⓗ level need to recognise the genitive in listening and reading papers and know what it means.

Nominative

The **nominative** case describes the noun or pronoun who/which does the action. This is the **subject** of the verb and is frequently at the start of the sentence.

Ich bin dreizehn Jahre alt und wohne in England. *I am thirteen years old and live in England.*

Der Junge macht heute Abend seine Hausaufgaben. *The boy is doing his homework this evening.*

Wir spielen dreimal pro Woche Fußball. *We play football three times a week.*

With inverted word order, the subject is placed as the third element or idea in a sentence, directly after the verb.

Heute Abend macht der Junge seine Hausaufgaben. *This evening the boy is doing his homework.*

Dreimal pro Woche spielen wir Fußball. *Three times a week we play football.*

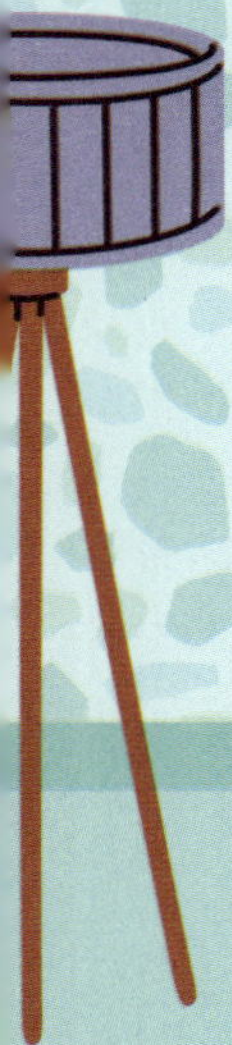

Accusative

The **accusative** case indicates the person or thing which is the **direct object** of the action. Most verbs are followed by the accusative form of nouns, including: **haben** *to have* and **es gibt** *there is/are*.

Ich habe eine Katze und einen Fisch.
I have a cat and a fish.

Ich besuche meine Schwester jeden Monat in Berlin. *I visit my sister every month in Berlin.*

Meine Eltern finden das Hotel bequem.
My parents find the hotel comfortable.

Dative

The **dative** case refers to the person or thing which is the **indirect object** of the action ('to' or 'for' someone or something).

Ich gebe meinem Freund ein Geschenk.
I am giving my friend a present. / I am giving a present to my friend.

Sie schreibt ihrer Mutter eine SMS.
She is writing her mother a text message. / She is writing a text to her mother.

Diese Tasche gehört ihm.
This bag belongs to him.

Ⓗ Genitive

The **genitive** case shows a relationship between two nouns. The first noun is 'owned by' or depends on the noun in the genitive case.

Die Fenster des Hauses waren nicht geschlossen. *The windows of the house were not closed.*

Das Buch meiner Mutter ist nicht so interessant. *My mother's book is not so interesting.*

Ich höre die Musik dieses Sängers. *I am listening to this singer's music.*

+ Instead of the genitive, it is often possible to use **von** + dative:
die Fenster vom Haus *the windows of the house*

Definite articles ('the') in different cases

	Masculine	Feminine	Neuter	Plural
Nominative	der	die	das	die
Accusative	den	die	das	die
Dative	dem	der	dem	den
Ⓗ Genitive	des	der	des	der

Indefinite articles ('a', 'an') in different cases

	Masculine	Feminine	Neuter	Plural
Nominative	ein	eine	ein	–
Accusative	einen	eine	ein	–
Dative	einem	einer	einem	–
Ⓗ Genitive	eines	einer	eines	–

ADJECTIVES

When we want to say what a thing or person is like – short, good, light, etc, – we use adjectives. They are placed very close to the word they describe.

In German, when an adjective is placed after a noun and used with a conjugation of **sein**, no additional endings are required.

Die Person ist berühmt. *The person is famous.* **Der Betreuer ist freundlich.** *The carer is friendly.*

If an adjective appears before a noun, you need to add an **ending** to the adjective. The choice of endings depends on which article comes before it and whether the noun is in the nominative, accusative or dative case.

Definite article + adjective

Case	Masculine	Feminine	Neuter	Plural
Nominative	der freundliche Vater	die berühmte Person	das schöne Lied	die guten Freunde
Accusative	den freundlichen Vater	die berühmte Person	das schöne Lied	die guten Freunde
Dative	dem freundlichen Vater	der berühmten Person	dem schönen Lied	den guten Freunden

Indefinite article + adjective

Case	Masculine	Feminine	Neuter	Plural
Nominative	ein freundlicher Mann	eine große Stadt	ein kleines Theater	keine geduldigen Schüler
Accusative	einen freundlichen Mann	eine große Stadt	ein kleines Theater	keine geduldigen Schüler
Dative	einem freundlichen Mann	einer großen Stadt	einem kleinen Theater	keinen geduldigen Schülern

! In the dative plural, add an **-n** ending to all the nouns.

These same adjectival endings apply if there is no indefinite article, the only exception being in the plural: **geduldige Schüler** (nom.) **geduldige Schüler** (acc.) **geduldigen Schülern** (dat.)

Possessive adjectives

These are adjectives such as 'my', 'your' and 'our' that indicate possession or ownership. Use the correct form for the gender and number of the thing possessed.

Singular

		my	your (referring to singular you)	his/its/one's	her
Nominative	m	mein	dein	sein	ihr
	n	mein	dein	sein	ihr
	f/pl	meine	deine	seine	ihre
Accusative	m	meinen	deinen	seinen	ihren
	n	mein	dein	sein	ihr
	f/pl	meine	deine	seine	ihre
Dative	m/n	meinem	deinem	seinem	ihrem
	f	meiner	deiner	seiner	ihrer
	pl	meinen	deinen	seinen	ihren

Plural

		our	your (referring to plural you, informal)	their	your (referring to singular or plural you, formal)
Nominative	m	unser	euer	ihr	Ihr
	n	unser	euer	ihr	Ihr
	f/pl	unsere	eure / euere	ihre	Ihre
Accusative	m	unseren	euren	ihren	Ihren
	n	unser	euer	ihr	Ihr
	f/pl	unsere	eure / euere	ihre	Ihre
Dative	m/n	unserem	eurem	ihrem	Ihrem
	f	unserer	eurer	ihrer	Ihrer
	pl	unseren	euren / euere	ihren	Ihren

! These possessive adjectives correspond with the noun as the subject or object of the sentence: **Mein Großvater hat zwei Katzen.** *My grandfather has two cats.*

Ich liebe meinen Großvater. *I love my grandfather.*

Mein Bruder und ich gehen mit unserem Großvater ins Theater.

My brother and I are going with our grandfather to the theatre.

→

Demonstrative adjectives

These correspond to the English 'this', 'these', 'that' and 'those'. The German equivalent is **dies**- with endings that follow the pattern of an adjective with an indefinite article.

	This			These
	Masculine	**Feminine**	**Neuter**	**Plural**
Nominative	dieser	diese	dieses	diese
Accusative	diesen	diese	dieses	diese
Dative	diesem	dieser	diesem	diesen

Other common demonstratives use the same endings:

alle *all* **beide** *both* **einige** *some* **viele** *much / many* **wenige** *few*

Indefinite adjectives

These indefinite adjectives carry the same endings as demonstrative adjectives.

gleicher / gleiche / gleiches *same*
jeder / jede / jedes *each/every*
letzter / letzte / letztes *last*
nächster / nächste / nächstes *next*

Interrogative adjectives

The interrogative adjective **welch**- is a question word meaning 'which'. Its endings follow the pattern of an adjective with an indefinite article.

Welchen Stars folgst du auf sozialen Medien?
Which celebrities do you follow on social media?

In welche Stadt fahren wir morgen?
Which town are we travelling to tomorrow?

Comparatives and superlatives

These adjectival phrases show you are making a comparison: 'more expensive than', 'cleaner', 'as tall as', 'less difficult', etc.

Comparatives

more + adjective + than / adjective + -er + than	adjective + **-er** + **als**	**Johannes ist ehrlicher als sein Bruder.** *Johannes is more honest than his brother.*
less + adjective + than	**weniger** + adjective + **als**	**Heidi ist weniger sportlich als Susanne.** *Heidi is less sporty than Susanne.*
as + adjective + as	**so** + adjective + **wie**	**Mein Handy ist so neu wie dein Handy.** *My mobile phone is as new as your phone.*

→

Comparatives and superlatives continued

Comparatives continued

Some comparative adjectives change their spelling: it can be the order of the letters, or the addition of an extra letter, or adding an umlaut on the **a**, **o** or **u**.

dunkel → dunkler *darker*	**lang → länger** *longer*
gesund → gesünder *healthier*	**nah → näher** *nearer, closer*
groß → größer *bigger*	**stark → stärker** *stronger*
jung → jünger *younger*	**teuer → teurer** *more expensive*
kalt → kälter *colder*	**warm → wärmer** *warmer*
kurz → kürzer *shorter*	

Ⓗ Superlatives

Superlatives are the highest form of comparison: 'the most expensive', 'the cleanest', etc.

the most + adjective / the + adjective + -est	definite article (case-dependent) + adjective + **-ste**

The **-ste** ending is the same for all singular nouns in the nominative case. When positioned before the noun, it follows the same pattern of endings as adjectives, in the accusative, dative and genitive cases – see **page 140**.

Dieser Film ist der lustigste. *This film is the funniest.*

Ich habe den schönsten Pullover gekauft. *I bought the nicest jumper.*

Irregular comparative and superlative forms

These common irregular forms are useful to know.

besser	*better*
höher	*higher*
der / die / das beste + noun, **am besten**	*the best*
der / die / das meiste + noun, **am meisten**	*the most*
der / die / das nächste + noun, **am nächsten**	*the next*

Es ist der beste Ort der Welt!
It's the best place in the world!

Diese Schuhe passen am besten zu meiner Hose.
These shoes suit my trousers best.

Expressing a preference

When you want to express a preference for something, use the adverb **lieber**. This comes directly after the verb in the clause.

Ich lerne lieber Deutsch.
I prefer learning German.

Meine Familie fährt lieber mit dem Auto. *My family prefers travelling by car.*

Wir gehen lieber heute als morgen ins Kino.
We prefer to go to the cinema today, not tomorrow.

ADVERBS

These are words that describe how the action of a verb is being done, such as 'carefully', 'slowly', 'often', 'fast'. They can also be used with an adjective: 'It was really delicious.'

In German, we can use adjectives as found in the dictionary as adverbs, with no additional endings.

Er spricht laut. *He is talking loudly.* **Sie singen schön.** *They sing beautifully.*

Ich fahre mein Fahrrad sehr langsam. *I am riding my bike very slowly.*

Time – Manner – Place

The adverbial elements of a sentence should be placed in this order: Time (**Wann**) – Manner (**Wie**) – Place (**Wo**).

! Even when a time phrase appears at the start of the sentence, all remaining elements are still organised around this principle.

Am Montag gehe ich zu Fuß in das Stadtzentrum.
On Monday I am going on foot to the town centre.

Adverbs of sequence

dann	*then*
danach	*next / afterwards*
also	*then / so*

Adverbs of place

drinnen	*inside*	dort	*there*
draußen	*outside*	nah	*near*
hier	*here*	weit	*far*

Adverbs of time and frequency

heute	*today*	übermorgen	*the day after tomorrow*
morgen	*tomorrow*	jetzt	*now*
gestern	*yesterday*	schon	*already*
immer	*always*	manchmal	*sometimes*
oft	*often*	nie	*never*

Adverbs of manner

allein	*alone / by oneself*
mit + dative noun	*with someone / something*

Quantifiers and intensifiers

sehr	*very*	ein bisschen	*a little / a bit*
genug	*enough*	viel / wenig	*a lot / little*
zu	*too*	ziemlich	*quite*

PRONOUNS

Subject pronouns

Subject pronouns are the words that refer to the person or thing doing the action of the verb. English examples: 'He is making the dinner.' 'We watched a film.' 'It isn't working.'

ich	*I*
du	*you (singular, informal)*
er	*he*
sie	*she*
es	*it*
man	*you, one, people in general*

wir	*we*
ihr	*you (plural, informal)*
sie*	*they*
Sie*	*you (plural or singular, formal)*

!

* These pronouns are differentiated from **sie** (*she*) through verb endings.

These pronouns mostly appear before a verb, instead of the name of a person or a thing. They appear after a verb when word order is inverted, to preserve the verb as the second idea.

Petra geht heute nicht in die Schule. Sie ist leider krank.
Heute geht Petra nicht in die Schule. Leider ist sie krank.
Petra is not going to school today. Unfortunately, she is ill.

Du, ihr, man and Sie

The pronouns **du**, **ihr**, **man** and **Sie** mean 'you'. It's essential to use the right one for the context!

Use **du** when addressing one person directly, often a friend or family member.
Was machst du morgen, Max? *What are you doing tomorrow, Max?*
Du hast keine Ahnung. *You have no idea.*

Use **ihr** when speaking to two or more people who you would normally address singly with **du**.
Ihr arbeitet jetzt zu zweit. *You (all) are now working in pairs / in twos.*

Use **man** when referring to a person or a general group of people within a particular situation.
Man wohnt im Urlaub oft in einem Hotel. *You often stay in a hotel on holiday.*
Man trägt beim Karneval ein Kostüm. *People wear a costume to the carnival.*

Use **Sie** with the third person plural of the verb to be extra respectful and polite to a singular person or a group of people, for example to a friend's parent, your school's headteacher, staff at a café, and to ask someone on the street for directions. Generally speaking, if you do not know the individual(s) personally, use **Sie** to address them.
Möchten Sie jetzt zahlen? *Would you like to pay now?*
Entschuldigen Sie bitte. *Excuse me, please.*

Direct object pronouns (accusative)

These are the pronouns that stand for things or people that are the **direct** object of the verb (i.e. what or who is receiving the action of the verb). In German, these relate to the **accusative** case.

mich	*me*
dich	*you (sing, informal)*
ihn	*him*
sie	*her*
es	*it*

uns	*us*
euch	*you (all) (pl, informal)*
sie	*them (pl)*
Sie	*you (sing / pl, formal)*

Ich habe dich gestern im Kino gesehen. *I saw you in the cinema yesterday.*

Mein Lehrer findet uns als Klasse lustig. *My teacher finds us funny as a class.*

Indirect object pronouns (dative)

These pronouns stand for things or people that are the **indirect** object of the verb. This means that they will have (or could have) the word 'to' in front of them. For example: 'He sent me a message.' (He sent a message **to me**.) In German, these correspond with the **dative** case.

mir	*(to) me*
dir	*(to) you (sing, informal)*
ihm	*(to) him / it*
ihr	*(to) her*

uns	*(to) us*
euch	*(to) you (all) (pl informal)*
ihnen	*(to) them (pl)*
Ihnen	*(to) you (sing / pl, formal)*

Er gab mir zum Geburtstag ein Geschenk. *He gave me a present for my birthday.*

Ich habe dir eine E-Mail geschrieben. *I wrote an email to you / I wrote you an email.*

Reflexive pronouns

These are the pronouns used with reflexive verbs (see **page 153**), verbs where the subject is the same as the object. A similar English verb is 'I enjoyed **myself**.'

Reflexive pronouns (accusative)

mich	*myself*
dich	*yourself (sing, informal)*
sich	*himself / herself / itself*

uns	*ourselves*
euch	*yourselves (pl, informal)*
sich	*themselves (pl) / yourselves (sing / pl, formal)*

Reflexive pronouns follow after the conjugated verb.

Ich kümmere mich um meinen Vater. *I am looking after my father.*

Hans entspannt sich jeden Abend. *Hans relaxes every evening.*

→

Reflexive pronouns continued

Reflexive pronouns (accusative) continued

H Higher

In a subordinate clause, the reflexive verb will go to the end, but the reflexive pronoun comes directly after the subject.

Ich denke, dass ich mich im Sommer entspannt habe.
I think that I relaxed in the summer.

Mein Freund ist cool, da wir uns beide für Musik interessieren. *My friend is cool, as we are both interested in music.*

+

You will know when a verb is reflexive because it will appear in vocabulary lists with **sich** before the infinitive, e.g. **sich interessieren für** *to be interested in*, **sich kümmern um** *to look after*.

Relative pronouns

Relative pronouns link phrases together, corresponding to the English 'who', 'which' or 'that' in the middle of a sentence (i.e. not when asking a question). For word order, see **page 156**.

	Masculine	Feminine	Neuter	Plural
Nominative	der	die	das	die
Accusative	den	die	das	die
H Dative	dem	der	dem	denen
H Genitive	dessen	deren	dessen	deren

Ich habe einen Bruder, der acht Jahre alt ist.
I have a brother, who is eight years old.

Die Frau, die ich sehe, liest ein Buch.
The woman (who) I see is reading a book.

!

Bear in mind that, in German, the relative pronoun is not optional like it is in English.
This is the dress (that) I bought yesterday.
Das ist das Kleid, das ich gestern gekauft habe.

H Higher

Using a relative pronoun with a preposition in the accusative, dative or genitive qualifies as a complex sentence. **Ich habe viele Freunde, mit denen ich tanzen gehe.** *I have lots of friends, with whom I go dancing.* (Here, **mit** takes the dative, and the relative pronoun relates to a plural noun.)

Pronominal adverbs

These are when the prefix **da** or **dar** combines with a preposition, making them a useful substitution for the preposition + 'it'.

Ich spiele mit dem Fußball. Ich spiele damit. *I am playing with the football. I am playing with it.*

Wir sprechen über die Stunde. Wir sprechen darüber. *We are talking about the lesson. We are talking about it.*

dadurch	*through (it)*	**davon**	*from (it)*
dahinter	*behind (it)*	**dafür**	*for (it)*
daneben	*next to (it)*	**damit**	*with (it)*
darüber	*over / about (it)*	**danach**	*after (it)*
dazwischen	*between (it)*	**davor**	*before (it)*

VERBS AND TENSES

The infinitive

The infinitive is the basic form of the verb, the starting point, and in English starts with 'to...'. For example, 'to make', 'to see', 'to be'.

In German, the majority of infinitives end with **-en**, e.g. **gehen** *to go*, **kaufen** *to buy*. An important exception to this pattern is **sein** *to be*. Other exceptions include **ändern** *to change*, **entwickeln** *to develop*, **lächeln** *to smile*.

The present tense

This tense is used for actions that are taking place now or take place regularly in the present time.

Heute Abend mache ich meine Hausaufgaben. *This evening, I am doing my homework.*

Ich wohne an der Küste. *I live on the coast.*

Die Stars machen viele Fotos. *Celebrities take lots of photos.*

The endings change depending on who is doing the action. Most verbs follow the pattern shown in the underlined letters in this table.

	lernen *to learn*	**machen** *to do, make*	**trinken** *to drink*
ich	lern<u>e</u>	mach<u>e</u>	trink<u>e</u>
du	lern<u>st</u>	mach<u>st</u>	trink<u>st</u>
er / sie / es / man	lern<u>t</u>	mach<u>t</u>	trink<u>t</u>
wir	lern<u>en</u>	mach<u>en</u>	trink<u>en</u>
ihr	lern<u>t</u>	mach<u>t</u>	trink<u>t</u>
sie / Sie	lern<u>en</u>	mach<u>en</u>	trink<u>en</u>

+

In German, the present tense is also used for the equivalent of English 'to be -ing' ('I am waiting', 'I am writing'), so **Ich gehe in die Schule** means both 'I go to school' and 'I am going to school'.

Common irregular verbs in the present tense

Make sure you know the full present tense for the following verbs: **haben** *to have*, **sein** *to be*, **werden** *to become*. These do not follow the regular pattern – see **page 162**.

Using the present tense with a future time phrase

Just as in English, you can use the present tense in German with an adverb of future time to talk about the future.

Morgen fahre ich nach Österreich.
Tomorrow I am travelling / I will travel to Austria.

Wir feiern nächste Woche ihre Hochzeit.
We are celebrating / We will celebrate their wedding next week.

The perfect tense

The perfect tense is used to say what you have done or what you did. For example, 'I have worked' or 'I worked'. In English, we use the verb 'to have' and a past participle, which usually ends in '-ed' but there are lots of irregulars, such as 'written', 'said', 'flown', 'caught'.

In German, the verbs **haben** and **sein** are used for 'to have' when forming the perfect tense.

Using haben to form the perfect tense

The majority of German verbs take **haben** in the perfect tense. Use the present tense of **haben**.

haben	
ich	habe
du	hast
er / sie / es / man	hat
wir	haben
ihr	habt
sie / Sie	haben

+

a past participle
The past participle of weak verbs follows a regular pattern: **ge-** + stem of verb **+ -t**
spielen → gespielt *played* **machen → gemacht** *did* **kaufen → gekauft** *bought*

Although the past participle is usually **ge-** + stem + **-t**, there are other common forms:

Past participle keeps the verb's inseparable prefix (instead of **ge-**)	**be-** e.g. **besucht** *visited*, **ent-** e.g. **entdeckt** *discovered*, **er-** e.g. **erzählt** *recounted*, **über-** e.g. **übersetzt** *translated*, **ver-** e.g. **versucht** *tried*, *attempted*
Past participle the same as the infinitive	**bekommen** *received*, *got*, **erfahren** *experienced*, **gefallen** *liked*, **vergessen** *forgotten*
Past participle **ge-** + infinitive	**gegeben** *given*, **gefahren** *went*, *travelled*
Irregular verb with a vowel change in the past participle	**ei → ie** e.g. **geblieben** *stayed*, *remained* **i → u** e.g. **gefunden** *found* **e → o** e.g. **gesprochen** *talked*, *spoken* **ie → o** e.g. **geflogen** *flew*

Using sein to form the perfect tense

Verbs of motion or transition use the present tense of **sein** to form the perfect tense.

sein	
ich	bin
du	bist
er / sie / es / man	ist
wir	sind
ihr	seid
sie / Sie	sind

+ **a past participle**

+ Irregular past participles are provided in the vocabulary list. You can use the verb tables on **pages 163-166** to check for the most common irregular verbs.

The perfect tense continued

These important verbs use **sein** to form the perfect tense:

bleiben *to stay*	**Ich bin in der Stadt geblieben.** *I stayed in town.*
fahren *to travel*	**Meine Familie ist mit dem Auto gefahren.** *My parents travelled by car.*
gehen *to go*	**Ich bin in die Schule gegangen.** *I went to school.*
schwimmen *to swim*	**Wir sind im Meer geschwommen.** *We swam in the ocean.*
sein *to be*	**Ich bin da gewesen.** *I have been there.*
werden *to become*	**Meine Mutter ist Journalistin geworden.** *My mother became a journalist.*

Using the perfect tense for past events

The German perfect tense is commonly used to refer to any past action or event.

Mein Bruder hat gestern seinen Freund getroffen. *My brother met up with his friend yesterday.*

Letzten Sommer habe ich in einem Café gearbeitet. *Last summer I worked in a café.*

! When translating from German into English, the appearance of the auxiliary verb (the conjugated form of **haben** or **sein**) can make it difficult to decide which English form is more appropriate ('I did' or 'I have done'). Think about the context and what sounds best in English, e.g. **Gestern habe ich bei mir Essen gekocht.** *Yesterday I cooked food at mine* sounds more idiomatic than *Yesterday I have cooked food at mine*.

The perfect tense + früher

If you want to say something you used to do habitually, you can use the word **früher** (*earlier, back then*) as an adverbial time phrase in your perfect tense sentence.

Ich habe früher viel mehr Sport gemacht.
I used to do much more sport back then.

Meine Eltern sind früher ins Ausland gereist.
My parents used to travel abroad back then.

Ⓗ Higher

Add variety to your work by using the **imperfect tense** for habitual events from the past.

The imperfect tense

The imperfect tense (or the simple past tense) is used to refer to a specific event in the past. It is also used to describe what something was like, and for repeated actions, i.e. to say things like *It was great. It was boring. I used to go to the gym. I used to work in the summer.*

The imperfect of haben and sein

The most useful verbs to know in the imperfect are **haben** and **sein**. You can use their imperfect forms to express things like 'I had', 'I used to have', 'I was', 'I used to be', 'it was ...'

	haben *to have*	**sein** *to be*
ich	hatte	war
du	hattest	warst
er / sie / es / man	hatte	war
wir	hatten	waren
ihr	hattet	wart
sie / Sie	hatten	waren

H Forming the imperfect tense of other verbs

Other verbs follow these patterns in the imperfect tense.

	Regular verbs	**Irregular verbs** (Often with a vowel change in the stem)
	kochen *to cook*	**bleiben** *to stay*
ich	kochte	blieb
du	kochtest	bliebst
er / sie / es / man	kochte	blieb
wir	kochten	blieben
ihr	kochtet	bliebt
sie / Sie	kochten	blieben

The future tense

This tense is equivalent to the English 'going to ...' and 'will ...'. It expresses what you are going to do / what is going to happen, and what you will do / what will happen.

The future tense in German is formed with the present tense of **werden** (**werde**, **wirst**, **wird**, **werden**, **werdet**, **werden**) + an infinitive. As the infinitive is the 'second verb', this will follow German word order rules and appear at the end of the clause.

Ich werde morgen einkaufen gehen. *I am going shopping tomorrow. / I will go shopping tomorrow.*

Sie wird nächstes Jahr im Ausland studieren. *She is going to study abroad next year. / She will study abroad next year.*

Modal verbs

Modal verbs express concepts such as ability, permission, necessity, possibility and obligation. They are often paired with an infinitive of another verb, which appears at the end of the clause.

> **!** **Ich möchte** / *would like* is actually the conditional form of modal verb **mögen** – but just learn it and you don't need to know the grammatical terminology to ask for something you'd like!
>
> **Ich möchte ein Eis.** *I'd like an ice cream.*
>
> **Möchtest du schwimmen gehen?** *Would you like to go swimming?*
>
> **Morgen möchten wir ausgehen.** *Tomorrow we would like to go out.*

Present tense

	dürfen *to be allowed to*	**können** *can / to be able to*	**mögen** *to like to*	**müssen** *must / to have to*	**sollen** *ought to*	**wollen** *to want to*
ich	darf	kann	mag	muss	soll	will
du	darfst	kannst	magst	musst	sollst	willst
er / sie / es / man	darf	kann	mag	muss	soll	will
wir	dürfen	können	mögen	müssen	sollen	wollen
ihr	dürft	könnt	mögt	müsst	sollt	wollt
sie / Sie	dürfen	können	mögen	müssen	sollen	wollen

Imperfect / Simple past tense

	dürfen *to be allowed to*	**können** *can / to be able to*	**mögen** *to like to*	**müssen** *must / to have to*	**sollen** *ought to*	**wollen** *to want to*
ich	durfte	konnte	mochte	musste	sollte	wollte
du	durftest	konntest	mochtest	musstest	solltest	wolltest
er / sie / es / man	durfte	konnte	mochte	musste	sollte	wollte
wir	durften	konnten	mochten	mussten	sollten	wollten
ihr	durftet	konntet	mochtet	musstet	solltet	wolltet
sie / Sie	durften	konnten	mochten	mussten	sollten	wollten

Ⓗ Conditional clauses

Conditional clauses express what you would or should do, or what would or should happen. They use a form called the imperfect subjunctive. You need to know the forms for **haben** (**ich hätte**) and **sein** (**ich wäre**).

To say what you would do, use the conditional form of **werden**: **ich würde** *I would* + an infinitive.

Ich würde morgen entweder Musik hören oder fernsehen. *Tomorrow I would either listen to music or watch TV.*

Meine Eltern würden das nie machen. *My parents would never do that.*

The conditional form of **sollen**: **ich sollte** *I should* + infinitive expresses what you should do or what should happen.

Ich sollte dahin gehen. *I should go there.*

Meine Schwester sollte dieses Museum besuchen. *My sister should visit this museum.*

Ⓗ The imperative

The imperative is used to give instructions or commands, and it only exists in the second person forms of the verb ('you').

For the **du** form, simply use the verb stem without endings, and add -**e**. However, the -**e** is often dropped in spoken German.

Hör(e) zu! *Listen!* **Beschreib(e) deine Familie.** *Describe your family.*

For some verb stems, you must keep the -**e** to help make the imperative easier to pronounce.

Öffne die Tür! *Open the door.* **Recycle deine Flaschen!** *Recycle your bottles!*

For the **ihr** form, use the verb stem in the infinitive and add -**t**.

Schreibt vier Sätze. *Write four sentences.*

Only in the **Sie** form of the imperative does the pronoun appear.

Machen Sie das sofort, bitte. *Do it immediately, please.*

Reflexive verbs

These verbs can be recognised because they have **sich** before the infinitive. They often describe actions that you do to yourself, e.g.
sich waschen *to have a wash*,
sich interessieren für *to be interested in*,
sich anziehen *to put on clothes / to dress yourself*.

Reflexive verbs follow the same endings in the present tense as the conjugation of weak and strong verbs. Some reflexive verbs are irregular.

Reflexive verbs are followed by a reflexive pronoun, most commonly in the accusative form.

	sich waschen *to have a wash*
ich	wasche mich
du	wäschst dich
er / sie / es / man	wäscht sich
wir	waschen uns
ihr	wascht euch
sie / Sie	waschen sich

Impersonal verbs

The most common impersonal verb phrases are **es gibt** ('there is/are') and **es gab** ('there was/were'). The noun that follows them is in the accusative case.

In meiner Stadt gibt es einen Supermarkt. *In my town there is a supermarket.*

Es gab keine bessere Möglichkeit. *There was no better option.*

Infinitive constructions

Use **um … zu …** to express 'in order to'. Other details always go between **um** and **zu**, and then the infinitive at the end of the clause.

Ich spiele jeden Tag Fußball, um fit zu bleiben. *I play football every day (in order) to stay healthy.*

Wir gehen jetzt ins Kino, um einen guten Platz zu finden. *We are going to the cinema now (in order) to get a good seat.*

Ⓗ Higher

Other infinitive constructions you can use are:

ohne … zu … *without* + verb **-ing**   **statt … zu …** *instead of* + verb **-ing**

Grammar

WORD ORDER

The order of words in a German sentence is very important. How the information is organised emphasises certain sections of the sentence.

Whatever else happens in a sentence, the verb must be the second idea. This does not always mean the second word, but the second element. (It's different in a 'yes-no' question – see page 159.)

Main clause word order

A **clause** is a segment of a sentence with a conjugated verb (related to its subject). It might be a standalone sentence or a part of a longer sentence.

One-verb rule

1 – Subject	2 – Verb	3	4
Ich	habe	in meiner Familie	drei Schwestern
Mein Bruder	geht	heute	ins Kino
Wir	lernen	mit der Klasse	Deutsch

→

Main clause word order continued

One-verb rule continued

If another element comes at the start (in position 1), we invert (swap over) the subject and verb, so that the verb is still the second idea (in position 2).

1	2 – Verb	3 – Subject	4
In meiner Familie	habe	ich	drei Schwestern
Heute	geht	mein Bruder	ins Kino
Mit der Klasse	lernen	wir	Deutsch

Two-verb rule

If there are two verbs or two parts of a verb in the main clause, the second one goes to the end of the clause.

1	2 – Verb	3	4	5 – Verb
Ich	habe	gestern	in der Küche	gekocht
Man	soll	jeden Tag	zu Hause	lesen
Morgen	wird	Daniel	mit Freunden	spielen

Information related to the second verb should come just before it in the clause.

1	2 – Verb	3	4	5 – Verb
Ich	habe	gestern	in der Küche	Essen gekocht
Man	soll	jeden Tag	zu Hause	ein Buch lesen
Morgen	wird	Daniel	mit Freunden	Tennis spielen

! Notice that the order of the elements follows the Time – Manner – Place rule. See **page 144** for more on this.

Separable verb word order

In the present tense, the **prefix** of a separable verb splits off from the **stem** of the verb and goes to the end of the clause.

1	2	3	4
ankommen *to arrive*			
Ich	komme	heute Abend	an
hochladen *to upload*			
Wir	laden	die Fotos	hoch
mitnehmen *to take with*			
Meine Eltern	nehmen	ihre Handys	mit

... ***Main clause word order*** **continued**

Word order with conjunctions: und, denn, aber

You can link two clauses with a **conjunction** (also known as a **connective**). Using **und** (*and*), **denn** (*because*) or **aber** (*but*) keeps the word order in each main clause the same.

Ich finde meine Brüder lustig, aber sie sind sehr faul.
I find my brothers funny, but they are very lazy.

Die Lehrerin mag ihren Beruf und hat mit den Schülern Spaß.
The teacher likes her job and has fun with the pupils.

Word order with other conjunctions

A **subordinate clause** connects to the **main clause** with a **subordinating conjunction**, often separated by a comma. The **verb** in the **subordinate clause** moves to the end.

bevor	*before*	(H) ob	*whether*
da	*as*	obwohl	*although*
(H) damit	*so that*	weil	*because*
dass	*that*	wenn	*when / if*

1 – Main clause + comma	2 – Subordinating conjunction	3 – Subordinate clause	4 – Subordinate clause verb
Ich arbeite heute nicht,	weil	ich krank	bin
Ich denke,	dass	soziale Medien praktisch	sind
Das Konzert war gut,	obwohl	die Band zu laut gespielt	hat

! Sentences with multiple clauses are complex. It is important to practise them to gain additional marks in your speaking and writing exams.

(H) Word order with relative pronouns

Relative pronouns are the little words that refer back to the subject in the main clause. They correspond in English to 'who', 'which' or 'that'. When you use them in German, the verb goes to the end of the clause.

	Masculine	Feminine	Neuter	Plural
Nominative: referring to the subject	der	die	das	die
Accusative: referring to the direct object	den	die	das	die

In der Schule gibt es viele Lehrer, die intelligent sind. *At school there are lots of teachers who are intelligent.*

Das Buch, das ich lese, ist ziemlich interessant. *The book that I am reading is quite interesting.*

Morgen mache ich die Hausaufgaben, die ich schwierig finde. *Tomorrow I will do the homework that I find difficult.*

PREPOSITIONS

Prepositions link a noun, pronoun or infinitive to another element in the sentence.

Prepositions affect the article ('the' or 'a') that is used with the noun, so you need to check you are using the correct form of that article, direct (**accusative**) or indirect (**dative**).

Prepositions with the accusative

bis	*until, as far as*	gegen	*against, towards, about (time-wise)*
durch	*through*	ohne	*without*
für	*for*	um	*around (a place), at (a time)*

Prepositions with the dative

außer	*except for*	nach	*after, to(wards)*
aus	*out of, originating from, made of*	seit	*since / for (period of past time)*
bei	*at the (house / shop) of, in the event of ...*	von	*of, from, by*
mit	*with*	zu	*to, at*

Prepositions with the dative or accusative

an	*at (the side of), on*	über	*over, about, via*
auf	*on (top of)*	unter	*under, among*
hinter	*behind*	vor	*before, in front of*
in	*in(to), in(side)*	zwischen	*between*
neben	*next to*		

When the sentence indicates **motion**, you would use these prepositions with the **accusative**.

Ich lege meine Tasche auf den Tisch.
I am putting my bag on(to) the table.

When the sentence refers to a **static position**, you would use these prepositions with the **dative**.

Meine Tasche liegt auf dem Tisch. *My bag is on the table.*

Contracted prepositions

When the prepositions **an**, **bei**, **in**, **von** and **zu** are used in the accusative and dative, they can merge with the **definite article** into a contracted form.

an das → ans	**ans Meer gehen** *to go to the sea*
an dem → am	**am Montag** *on Monday*
bei dem → beim	**beim Großvater wohnen** *to live at your grandfather's*
in das → ins	**ins Konzert gehen** *to go to a classical concert*
in dem → im	**im Sommer** *in the summer*
von dem → vom	**vom Platz** *from the square*
zu dem → zum	**zum Flughafen fahren** *to travel to the airport*
zu der → zur	**zur Schule gehen** *to go to school*

Verbs followed by prepositions

Many German verbs must be followed by a particular preposition. The preposition does not always correspond to the English equivalent, so you will need to learn them. For example, note the contrast between **für** and English *in* in this sentence:

Sie interessiert sich für deutsche Filme.
She is interested in German films.

ankommen an + dat. noun	*to arrive at*
auskommen mit + dat. noun	*to get on with*
denken an + acc. noun	*to think of*
erzählen von + dat. noun	*to tell about*
gehen um + acc. noun	*to be about*
hoffen auf + acc. noun	*to hope for*
sich interessieren für + acc. noun	*to be interested in*
schützen vor + dat. noun	*to protect from*
sich kümmern um + acc. noun	*to take care of*

Seit and vor

Seit means 'since' or 'for', in the sense of a period of time. To say how long you have been or were doing something, use **seit** + a period of time, followed by the verb in the present tense.

Vor means 'ago'.

When you use these, remember the word order is different from English.

Seit zwei Jahren esse ich kein Fleisch.
I have not eaten meat for two years.

Seit einem Monat studiert Sylvie an der Uni.
Sylvie has been studying at uni for a month.

Vor drei Wochen bin ich ins Kino gegangen.
I went to the cinema three weeks ago.

Vor einem Jahr hat Tanja neue Schuhe gekauft.
Tanja bought new shoes a year ago.

QUESTIONS

A 'yes-no' question can be asked in German by inverting the verb and the subject. Put the verb first, then the subject (the name or pronoun).

Mareike spielt jeden Tag Tennis. *Mareike plays tennis every day.*

Spielt Mareike jeden Tag Tennis? *Does Mareike play tennis every day?*

Sie spielt manchmal Fußball. *She sometimes plays football.*

Spielt sie manchmal Fußball? *Does she sometimes play football?*

Question words

Another way to ask a question in German is to use a question word. Start with that; then the verb has to come next, i.e. place the verb before the subject, to keep the verb as the second idea.

Wo wohnt Julian? *Where does Julian live?*

Wann kommst du uns besuchen? *When are you coming to visit us?*

It is really important to learn the question words, especially for the speaking exam.

Most common question words

Wann ...?	*When ...?*
Warum ...?	*Why ...?*
Was ...?	*What ...?*
Was für ...?	*What sort of ...?*
Welcher / Welche / Welches ...?	*Which (m / f / nt) ...?*
Wer / Wen / Wem ...?*	*Who ...?*
Wie ...?	*How ...?*
Wie viel(e) ...?	*How much / many ...?*
Um wie viel Uhr ...?	*At what time ...?*
Wo ...?	*Where ...?*

* The interrogative pronoun **wer** (*who*) has different forms that you need to use according to whether the person you are asking about is the subject, direct object or indirect object of the verb.

Nominative (subject)	Wer ...?	**Wer bist du?** *Who are you?*
Accusative (direct object)	Wen ...?	**Wen siehst du?** *Who can you see?*
Dative (indirect object)	Wem ...?	**Wem gehört diese Tasche?** *Who does this bag belong to? / To whom does this bag belong?*

NEGATION

Nicht

To make a sentence negative, the most common word used is **nicht**, meaning 'not'. This is usually placed before the word which it negates.

Ich verstehe nicht. *I don't understand.*

Ich finde dieses Kleid nicht schön. *I think this dress is not nice.*

Er kann mir nicht helfen. *He cannot help me.*

Das ist nicht für mich. *This is not for me.*

Kein

Use **kein** instead of **nicht ein** to express when there is 'none of' or 'nothing of' something.

Ich habe keine Karte. *I don't have a ticket.*

Es gibt von der Party keine Fotos. *There are no photos from the party.*

The different endings of **kein** follow the same pattern as endings for the indefinite article across the nominative, accusative and dative cases.

Other negative words

Other negative words will allow you to add complexity to your speaking and writing:

nie *never* **niemand** *nobody, no one* (subj) **niemanden** *nobody, no one* (obj)

Ⓗ Use the expression **nicht ... sondern ...** to say 'not ... but ...'.

Ich gehe heute nicht klettern, sondern schwimmen.
Today I am going not climbing but swimming.

Meine Mutter hat nicht nur Deutsch, sondern auch Spanisch gelernt.
My mother learned not only German but also Spanish.

VERB TABLES

Weak (regular) verbs

All weak verbs use the endings shown here for the present tense.

Infinitive: **lernen** *to learn*

	Present	Perfect	Imperfect	Future
ich	lerne	habe ... gelernt	lernte	werde ... lernen
du	lernst	hast ... gelernt	lerntest	wirst ... lernen
er / sie / es / man	lernt	hat ... gelernt	lernte	wird ... lernen
wir	lernen	haben ... gelernt	lernten	werden ... lernen
ihr	lernt	habt ... gelernt	lerntet	werdet ... lernen
sie / Sie	lernen	haben ... gelernt	lernten	werden ... lernen

Strong (semi-regular) verbs

These use the same present tense endings as weak verbs, but there are vowel changes in the verb stem, in the forms for **du** and **er/sie/es/man**.

Infinitive: **sprechen** *to speak*

	Present	Perfect*	Imperfect	Future
ich	spreche	habe ... gesprochen	sprach	werde ... sprechen
du	sprichst	hast ... gesprochen	sprachst	wirst ... sprechen
er / sie / es / man	spricht	hat ... gesprochen	sprach	wird ... sprechen
wir	sprechen	haben ... gesprochen	sprachen	werden ... sprechen
ihr	sprecht	habt ... gesprochen	spracht	werdet ... sprechen
sie / Sie	sprechen	haben ... gesprochen	sprachen	werden ... sprechen

*Remember that verbs of movement and transition take the conjugated form of **sein** instead of **haben** in the perfect tense – as in the example in the table below.

Infinitive: **bleiben** *to stay*

	Present	Perfect*
ich	bleibe	bin ... geblieben
du	bleibst	bist ... geblieben
er / sie / es / man	bleibt	ist ... geblieben
wir	bleiben	sind ... geblieben
ihr	bleibt	seid ... geblieben
sie / Sie	bleiben	sind ... geblieben

Key irregular verbs — haben, sein and werden

The present tense of these three verbs is absolutely essential to learn. You will often need **haben** and **sein**, to form the perfect tense, and you will need **werden** to form the future tense.

Imperfect tense

Ⓕ Foundation candidates only need to be familiar with a few key imperfect forms of two verbs: **haben** and **sein** (**ich hatte**, **ich war**, **es war**, etc.).

Ⓗ Higher candidates will need to learn the imperfect for certain verbs. These can be learned as vocabulary items and they appear in the AQA Higher vocabulary list. But to help you add complexity to your written and spoken work, the tables below list all the imperfect tense forms.

haben *to have*	Present	Perfect	Imperfect	Future
ich	habe	*Present tense of* **haben** + **gehabt** *e.g.* **ich habe gehabt**	hatte	*Present tense of* **werden** + **haben** *e.g.* **ich werde haben**
du	hast		hattest	
er / sie / es / man	hat		hatte	
wir	haben		hatten	
ihr	habt		hattet	
sie / Sie	haben		hatten	

sein *to be*	Present	Perfect	Imperfect	Future
ich	bin	*Present tense of* **sein** + **gewesen** *e.g.* **ich bin gewesen**	war	*Present tense of* **werden** + **sein** *e.g.* **ich werde sein**
du	bist		warst	
er / sie / es / man	ist		war	
wir	sind		waren	
ihr	seid		wart	
sie / Sie	sind		waren	

werden *to become*	Present	Perfect	Ⓗ Imperfect	Future
ich	werde	*Present tense of* **sein** + **geworden** *e.g.* **ich bin geworden**	wurde	*Present tense of* **werden** + **werden** *e.g.* **ich werde werden**
du	wirst		wurdest	
er / sie / es / man	wird		wurde	
wir	werden		wurden	
ihr	werdet		wurdet	
sie / Sie	werden		wurden	

Irregular verbs

beginnen *to begin*	Present	Perfect	Imperfect (H)	Future
ich	beginne	*Present tense of* **haben + begonnen**	begann	*Present tense of* **werden + beginnen**
du	beginnst		begannst	
er / sie / es / man	beginnt		begann	
wir	beginnen		begannen	
ihr	beginnt		begannt	
sie / Sie	beginnen		begannen	

bringen *to bring*	Present	Perfect	Imperfect (H)	Future
ich	bringe	*Present tense of* **haben + gebracht**	brachte	*Present tense of* **werden + bringen**
du	bringst		brachtest	
er / sie / es / man	bringt		brachte	
wir	bringen		brachten	
ihr	bringt		brachtet	
sie / Sie	bringen		brachten	

essen *to eat*	Present	Perfect	Imperfect (H)	Future
ich	esse	*Present tense of* **haben + gegessen**	aß	*Present tense of* **werden + essen**
du	isst		aßest	
er / sie / es / man	isst		aß	
wir	essen		aßen	
ihr	esst		aßt	
sie / Sie	essen		aßen	

fahren *to travel, go*	Present	Perfect	Imperfect (H)	Future
ich	fahre	*Present tense of* **sein + gefahren**	fuhr	*Present tense of* **werden + fahren**
du	fährst		fuhrst	
er / sie / es / man	fährt		fuhr	
wir	fahren		fuhren	
ihr	fahrt		fuhrt	
sie / Sie	fahren		fuhren	

finden *to find*	Present	Perfect	Imperfect (H)	Future
ich	finde	*Present tense of* **haben + gefunden**	fand	*Present tense of* **werden + finden**
du	findest		fandest	
er / sie / es / man	findet		fand	
wir	finden		fanden	
ihr	findet		fandet	
sie / Sie	finden		fanden	

Irregular verbs continued

geben *to give*	Present	Perfect	Ⓗ Imperfect	Future
ich	gebe	*Present tense of* **haben + gegeben**	gab	*Present tense of* **werden + geben**
du	gibst		gabst	
er / sie / es / man	gibt		gab	
wir	geben		gaben	
ihr	gebt		gabt	
sie / Sie	geben		gaben	

gehen *to go*	Present	Perfect	Ⓗ Imperfect	Future
ich	gehe	*Present tense of* **sein + gegangen**	ging	*Present tense of* **werden + gehen**
du	gehst		gingst	
er / sie / es / man	geht		ging	
wir	gehen		gingen	
ihr	geht		gingt	
sie / Sie	gehen		gingen	

gewinnen *to win*	Present	Perfect	Ⓗ Imperfect	Future
ich	gewinne	*Present tense of* **haben + gewonnen**	gewann	*Present tense of* **werden + gewinnen**
du	gewinnst		gewannst	
er / sie / es / man	gewinnt		gewann	
wir	gewinnen		gewannen	
ihr	gewinnt		gewannt	
sie / Sie	gewinnen		gewannen	

helfen *to help*	Present	Perfect	Ⓗ Imperfect	Future
ich	helfe	*Present tense of* **haben + geholfen**	half	*Present tense of* **werden + helfen**
du	hilfst		halfst	
er / sie / es / man	hilft		half	
wir	helfen		halfen	
ihr	helft		halft	
sie / Sie	helfen		halfen	

kommen *to come*	Present	Perfect	Ⓗ Imperfect	Future
ich	komme	*Present tense of* **sein + gekommen**	kam	*Present tense of* **werden + kommen**
du	kommst		kamst	
er / sie / es / man	kommt		kam	
wir	kommen		kamen	
ihr	kommt		kamt	
sie / Sie	kommen		kamen	

Irregular verbs continued

lesen *to read*	Present	Perfect	Ⓗ Imperfect	Future
ich	lese	*Present tense of* **haben + gelesen**	las	*Present tense of* **werden + lesen**
du	liest		last / lasest	
er / sie / es / man	liest		las	
wir	lesen		lasen	
ihr	lest		last / laset	
sie / Sie	lesen		lasen	

nehmen *to take*	Present	Perfect	Ⓗ Imperfect	Future
ich	nehme	*Present tense of* **haben + genommen**	nahm	*Present tense of* **werden + nehmen**
du	nimmst		nahmst	
er / sie / es / man	nimmt		nahm	
wir	nehmen		nahmen	
ihr	nehmt		nahmt	
sie / Sie	nehmen		nahmen	

sehen *to see, watch*	Present	Perfect	Ⓗ Imperfect	Future
ich	sehe	*Present tense of* **haben + gesehen**	sah	*Present tense of* **werden + sehen**
du	siehst		sahst	
er / sie / es / man	sieht		sah	
wir	sehen		sahen	
ihr	seht		saht	
sie / Sie	sehen		sahen	

schwimmen *to swim*	Present	Perfect	Ⓗ Imperfect	Future
ich	schwimme	*Present tense of* **sein + geschwommen**	schwamm	*Present tense of* **werden + schwimmen**
du	schwimmst		schwammst	
er / sie / es / man	schwimmt		schwamm	
wir	schwimmen		schwammen	
ihr	schwimmt		schwammt	
sie / Sie	schwimmen		schwammen	

tragen *to wear*	Present	Perfect	Ⓗ Imperfect	Future
ich	trage	*Present tense of* **haben + getragen**	trug	*Present tense of* **werden + tragen**
du	trägst		trugst	
er / sie / es / man	trägt		trug	
wir	tragen		trugen	
ihr	tragt		trugt	
sie / Sie	tragen		trugen	

Irregular verbs continued

trinken *to drink*	Present	Perfect	Imperfect (H)	Future
ich	trinke	*Present tense of* **haben + getrunken**	trank	*Present tense of* **werden + trinken**
du	trinkst		trankst	
er / sie / es / man	trinkt		trank	
wir	trinken		tranken	
ihr	trinkt		trankt	
sie / Sie	trinken		tranken	

wissen *to know*	Present	Perfect	Imperfect (H)	Future
ich	weiß	*Present tense of* **haben + gewusst**	wusste	*Present tense of* **werden + wissen**
du	weißt		wusstest	
er / sie / es / man	weiß		wusste	
wir	wissen		wussten	
ihr	wisst		wusstet	
sie / Sie	wissen		wussten	

EXAMINATION PRACTICE ANSWERS

For detail on how the exam will be marked, you can download the mark schemes from the AQA website and marking guidance from ClearRevise.com.

Theme 1 People and lifestyle

Reading

01 B 02 A 03 B 04 A 05 C [5 marks]

06 M + G 07 M + G 08 M 09 G 10 M 11 G [6 marks]

Listening

01 B 02 E 03 D 04 H 05 A 06 G [6 marks]

	Model answer	Accept	Reject	Mark
07	had to do all subjects / had no choice	had to learn all subjects		1
08	some of her friends would do no exercise	some friends wouldn't do any sport		1
09	homework three times a week	three lots of homework a week		1
10	water sports other activities / climbing	aquatic sports activities in open air		1 1

Dictation [10 marks]

11 Ich werde im September vier Fächer wählen.
12 Wir tragen als Uniform eine gelbe Krawatte.
13 Gekochte Eier sind lecker.
14 Meine Schwester will jetzt weniger Fleisch essen.
15 Der Unterricht in der Schule ist unglaublich schwierig.

Speaking

Role play

Examples of answers and marks awarded: [10 marks]

	2 marks	1 mark	0 marks
01	Mein Freund/Meine Freundin hat blonde Haare.	Schlank.	Freund gross (mispronunciation of **groß**)
02	Er/Sie ist freundlich.	Lustig.	Verstanden.
03	Mir gefällt die Schule.	Gefällt die Schule.	goote Schoole (mispronunciation of **gute Schule**)
04	Mein Lieblingsfach ist Mathe.	Lieblingsfach Englisch.	Deutschland.
05	Beschreibe deine Familie.	Große Familie?	Familie?

Reading aloud task (5 marks; conversation 10 marks)

06 Check your pronunciation by listening to the **recording**. [5 + 10 marks]

Photo card

07 Response to content of photos [5 marks]
Listen to the **recording** to hear an example of a student talking about the two photos.

08 Photo card unprepared conversation [20 marks]

Writing

01 Translation into **English** [10 marks]

	German	Model answer	Accept	Reject	Mark
01.1	Ich bin sehr glücklich,	I am very lucky	really lucky		1
	Ingrid als Freundin zu haben.	to have Ingrid as a friend.	to have a friend/ girlfriend like Ingrid		1
01.2	Sie ist sehr lieb	She is very kind	really nice/dear		1
	und hört mir zu.	and listens to me.		listens on its own	1
01.3	Ein guter Freund ist	A good friend is			1
	immer für dich da.	always there for you.			1
01.4	Wir teilen unsere Interessen	We share our interests		interests on its own	1
	und lachen zusammen.	and laugh together.			1
01.5	Sie ist sehr ehrlich	She is very honest	truthful		1
	und lügt nie.	and never lies.			1

02 Translation into **German**. [10 marks]

	English	Model answer	Accept	Reject	Mark
02.1	He has brown hair	Er hat braune Haare			1
	and he wears glasses.	und er trägt eine Brille.			1
02.2	Sometimes I fight	Ich streite mich manchmal	Manchmal streite ich mich		1
	with my brother.	mit meinem Bruder.			1
02.3	I am going to study	Ich werde ... studieren.			1
	three subjects next year.	nächstes Jahr drei Fächer			1
02.4	You do not have to study	Man muss ... lernen.	studieren		1
	all subjects.	nicht alle Fächer		Incorrect word order of nicht	1
02.5	I hate our uniform –	Ich hasse unsere Uniform –			1
	it is very ugly.	sie ist sehr hässlich.			1

03 **90**-word writing task (Foundation and Higher) [15 marks]

Example:

Ich esse gern Fisch und koche ihn mindestens zweimal pro Woche zu Hause. Ich esse auch gern Hähnchen. Man kann viel mit Hähnchen kochen und alle Gerichte sind sehr lecker. Ich bin kein Vegetarier, denn ich mag Fleisch. Manchmal probiere ich auch vegetarisches Essen.

Ich werde nächste Woche mit Freunden im Park Fußball spielen und am Sonntag ins Schwimmbad gehen, um gesund zu bleiben.

Letzte Woche bin ich mit Freunden und meinem Hund auf dem Land spazieren gegangen. Wir sind zwanzig Kilometer zu Fuß gelaufen und haben zusammen gegessen. **[89 words]**

04 **150**-word writing task (Higher tier) [25 marks]

Example:

Normalerweise gehe ich um Viertel vor neun zur Schule und der Unterricht beginnt um neun Uhr. Wir haben zwei Stunden vor der Pause. In der Pause kaufe ich etwas von dem Imbiss in der Stadt und rede mit Freunden. Danach haben wir Unterricht bis halb eins. Wir essen draußen im Schulhof oder in der Kantine zu Mittag. Das Essen ist nicht schlecht, aber es gibt fast jeden Tag Kartoffel! Nach der Pause habe ich zwei Stunden und dann ist der Schultag um fünfzehn Uhr zu Ende.

Nächstes Jahr werde ich an meiner Schule bleiben, um Abitur zu machen. Man muss drei Fächer wählen. Ich möchte sicherlich Englisch und Theater machen und versuche, entweder Geschichte oder Kunst zu wählen. Nach zwei Jahren gehe ich hoffentlich an die Uni. Aber im Moment interessiere ich mich nicht für eine Karriere. Vielleicht könnte ich eine Ausbildung machen. **[143 words]**

Theme 2 Popular culture

Reading

01 V 02 E 03 V 04 C 05 T 06 E 07 C 08 C

	German	Model answer	Accept	Reject	Mark
09	Ich lese	I read / I am reading			1
	in meinem Schlafzimmer.	in my bedroom.	room		1
10	Letzte Woche	Last week			1
	bin ich schwimmen gegangen.	I went swimming.	I swam		1
11	Als Kind bin ich sehr oft ... gegangen.	As a child I often went			1
	mit meinen Eltern ins Kino	to the cinema with my parents.			1
12	Man sollte ... anziehen.	One/You/People should wear	ought to		1
	für den Karneval ein Kostüm	a costume for carnival.	Carnival celebrations carnival		1
13	Manche Stars posten	Some stars post		A few Many	1
	zu viel auf sozialen Medien.	too much on social media.			1

Listening

01 P 02 N 03 P + N 04 N [4 marks]

05 A 06 A + B 07 A 08 A + B 09 A [5 marks]

Dictation [10 marks]

10.1 Als Basketballspieler bleibe ich aktiv und gesund.

10.2 Berühmte Leute haben manchmal zu viel Einfluss.

10.3 Traditionelle Feste sind meiner Meinung nach sehr kulturell.

10.4 Ich möchte ein traditionelles Fest auf dem Land besuchen.

10.5 Sportsendungen sind beliebt, aber ich folge ihnen nicht.

Speaking

Role play

Examples of answers and marks awarded:

	2 marks	1 mark	0 marks
01	Ich liebe ihn, weil man mit anderen spielen kann.	Ich liebe ihn. Mit anderen.	Ich mache Sport.
02	Ich spiele Gitarre, weil ich in einer Band bin.	Ich spiele Gitarre.	Ich mag Instrumente.
03	Ich bin / Wir sind ins Kino gegangen, um einen Film zu sehen.	Ich war im Kino.	Ich sehe Filme und esse Popcorn.
04	Es ist bequem und kostet nichts.	Es ist bequem. Mit anderen.	Bequem Hause.
05	Siehst du Sportsendungen? Wie findest du Sport im Fernsehen?	Sport im Fernsehen gut?	Sportsendungen sehen?

06 Response to content.
Listen to the **recording** to hear an example of a student talking about the two photos. [5 marks]

07 Unprepared conversation. [20 marks]

Writing

01 Examples of answers and marks awarded: [10 marks]

2 marks	1 mark	0 marks
Es gibt/Ich sehe vier/4 Personen. Es gibt/Ich sehe einige Freunde.	vier Personen einige Freunde	Vier (alone) Inappropriate verb + number of people, e.g. Es hat vier Freunde.
Sie wandern. Sie sind auf dem Land.	im Urlaub	
Sie lachen. Sie machen Fotos. Sie hat ein Handy. Sie trägt eine Jacke. Es gibt einen Mann. Es gibt eine Frau.	Fotos machen ein Handy	lachen (alone) Mann (alone)
Es gibt/Ich sehe Berge. Das Wetter ist schön. Es ist sonnig. Es ist heiß.	Berge schönes Wetter Sonnig	Inappropriate verb + adjective, e.g. Es hat sonnig. Ich bin Bergen. Ich möchte sonnig.
Die Frau lacht. Der Mann ist froh.	glüclkliche Frau froher Mann	lachen (alone) froh (alone)

02 Translation into **German**. [10 marks]

	English	Model answer	Accept	Reject
02.1	I am cooking	Ich koche		
	dinner for my parents.	Abendessen für meine Eltern.	für meine Eltern zu Abend.	
02.2	I played guitar	Ich habe ... Gitarre gespielt.		
	last night	gestern Abend	letzte Nacht	
	for an audience.	für ein Publikum	Zuschauer	
02.3	After the festival	Nach dem Fest		
	you can go	kann man ... gehen.	kannst du ... gehen non-inverted verb	
	to the beach.	zum Strand		am Strand
02.4	I never watch	Ich sehe nie	Ich schaue mir nie ... an.	
	documentaries	Dokumentarfilme		
	on TV.	im Fernsehen.		fern
02.5	I think that	Ich denke, dass	Ich denke,	
	celebrities should be	Stars ... sein sollten.	Stars sollten ... sein.	
	good role models	gute Vorbilder		Vorbild (singular)
	to young people.	für junge Leute	Jugendliche	

03 **90**-word writing task (Foundation and Higher) [15 marks]

Example:

Ich werde nächstes Jahr sechzehn Jahre alt, und ich möchte eine große Feier haben, um meinen Geburtstag zu feiern. Ich möchte auch leckeres Essen für alle kochen und mit meinen Freunden tanzen. Das wäre super.

Ich gehe am Wochenende gern mit meiner Familie spazieren, aber ich gehe lieber mit meinen Freunden aus. Wir interessieren uns für die gleichen Sachen, wie Kino und Musik, und wir streiten uns nie.

Letzte Woche bin ich meinem Lieblingsstar auf sozialen Medien gefolgt. Er spielt Tennis und ist international sehr bekannt. Er hat aber über seine Frau etwas Negatives geschrieben. Das war schrecklich und unhöflich. **[100 words]**

04 **150**-word writing task (Higher tier) [25 marks]

Example:

Letztes Wochenende hatte ich viele Probleme und es war wirklich schrecklich. Ich war mit meinen Freunden in der Stadt und ich habe mein Handy verloren. Heutzutage ist Technologie für junge Leute sehr wichtig, also war es ohne Handy für mich sehr langweilig. Wir sind danach ins Kino gegangen, um eine Komödie zu sehen. Der Film war aber nicht lustig und ich hatte Hunger. Wir sind dann in ein italienisches Restaurant gegangen, aber das Essen war kalt und sehr teuer. Ein schlechter Tag!

Es gibt einige Persönlichkeiten, die für Jugendliche gute Vorbilder sind. Zum Beispiel mag ich Steffi Sonntag, weil sie eine fantastische Fußballspielerin ist und auch, weil sie immer mit allen freundlich und offen ist. Außerdem unterstützt sie Hilfsorganisationen und arbeitet oft mit Armen und der Jugend. Manche Stars haben aber zu viel Geld und geben es nur für teure Sachen aus. Meiner Meinung nach sind einige Stars über ihr Leben zu öffentlich. Deswegen liebe ich Steffi Sonntag, da ihr Leben privat bleibt. **[162 words]**

Theme 3 Communication and the world around us

Reading

01 P 02 P + N 03 N 04 P [4 marks]

	Model answer	Accept	Reject	Mark
05	A chance to do something together. You work as a team.			2
06	Be in nature. Forget problems from life in the town.			2
07	Build a new (school) classroom for the village. Take part in an environmental project.	Issues		2
08	**Either** Good friends **Or** A couple might get married			2
09	Winter sports			1
10	Hotels are more expensive	Can cost a lot more		1

Listening

01 P 02 P 03 P + N 04 P + N [4 marks]

05 4P 06 2F [2 marks]

Dictation [10 marks]

07 Ich wohne in einem Haus auf dem Land.

08 Mein Handy ist ein sehr altes Gerät.

09 Unsere Welt ist vom Klimawandel bedroht.

10 Ich habe gestern die Fotos hochgeladen.

11 Meine Schwester wird zu Hause den Müll trennen.

Speaking

Role play

Examples of answers and marks awarded: [10 marks]

	2 marks	1 mark	0 marks
01.1	Ich fahre nach Griechenland, um meine Großeltern zu besuchen.	Nach Griechenland.	Familie in Griechen.
01.2	Ich habe das Hotelzimmer auf dem Computer reserviert.	Hotelzimmer auf dem Computer.	Technologie ist gut für Urlaub.
01.3	Ich fliege lieber mit dem Flugzeug, weil das schneller ist.	Bahn ist billiger.	Schnellerer Verkehr.
01.4	Wir spielen Fußball im Park und dann posten wir Fotos auf sozialen Medien.	Park und Fotos.	Ich liebe Sommerferien mit Freunden.
01.5	Wo wohnst du?	Dein Haus?	Wohnen?

Reading aloud task (5 marks; conversation 10 marks)

02 Check your pronunciation by listening to the **recording**. [5 + 10 marks]

Photo card

03 Response to content of photos [5 marks]

Listen to the **recording** to hear an example of a student talking about the two photos.

04 Photo card unprepared conversation [20 marks]

Listen to the **recording** to hear an example of a student answering the questions.

Writing

01 Translation into **German**. [10 marks]

	English	Model answer	Accept	Reject
01.1	I used the computer	Ich habe den Computer benutzt,		
	to buy	um ... zu kaufen.		
	the tickets.	die Tickets	Karten	
01.2	Lilian helps her grandfather	Lilian hilft ihrem Großvater,		
	to do his shopping	sein Einkäufe ... zu machen.	zu kaufen	
	online.	online		
01.3	He did	Er hat ... gemacht.	machte	
	his homework	seine Hausaufgaben		
	on his laptop.	auf seinem Laptop	an seinem Computer	Reference to gadget without his
01.4	Young people	Junge Leute		
	spend too much time	verbringen zu viel Zeit		
	on their mobile phones.	an ihren Handys.	an dem Handy, am Handy	
01.5	I forgot	Ich habe vergessen		
	to upload	... hochzuladen.		
	the photos.	die Fotos.		

02 **90**-word writing task (Foundation and Higher) [15 marks]

Example:

Ich mag es, wo ich wohne, und mir gefällt mein Leben hier. Es ist ruhig mit vielen Bäumen, aber es gibt auch Geschäfte, wo man gut einkaufen kann. Meine Freunde wohnen in der Nähe.

In den letzten Ferien bin ich mit meiner Familie nach Cornwall gefahren. Wir haben in einem Haus an der Küste direkt am Strand gewohnt. Es war sehr heiß und wir konnten jeden Tag im Meer schwimmen.

In der Zukunft möchte ich gern in die Schweiz fahren. Ich denke, dass sie ein fantastisches Land mit vielen interessanten Traditionen und Festen ist. Außerdem liebe ich Ski fahren. **[99 words]**

03 **150**-word writing task (Higher tier) [25 marks]

Example:

Ich mache mir Sorgen über Umweltprobleme, weil sie überall zu sehen sind, nicht nur in meinem Gebiet, sondern auf der ganzen Welt. Wo ich wohne, ist der Verkehr ein großes Problem. Es gibt zu viele Autos und man kann die Luftverschmutzung nicht vermeiden. Der Klimawandel hat große Folgen für alle. Wenn die Temperaturen steigen, ändert sich das Leben von Menschen und besonders von Tieren. Ich finde es sehr wichtig, Tierarten zu schützen.

In der Schule lernen wir viel über die Umwelt und versuchen immer, Energie zu sparen. Wir machen immer das Licht aus. Wir sammeln Plastikflaschen und recyceln Papier und Glas. Jedes Jahr haben wir einen Tag, wenn wir zu Fuß in die Schule gehen oder mit dem Fahrrad zur Schule fahren und Projekte zum Müllsammeln organisieren. Letztes Weihnachten haben meine Familie und ich zum Weihnachtsessen kein Fleisch gekocht. Wir versuchen jetzt, mehr vegetarisches Essen zu essen, weil es besser für die Umwelt ist. **[154 words]**

GUIDANCE ON GETTING TOP MARKS

+ Download pack

A full online version of this guidance gives you more advice on how to develop your answers progressively through the full range of marks. Download the complete pack from **ClearRevise.com**

Listening exam | Paper 1

Ⓕ Foundation and Ⓗ Higher tiers | Full marks

In **Section A** of the exam, questions will either be multiple choice or they will need to be answered in English. In **Section B** you will have a dictation task where you need to write down what you hear in German. For the dictation there will be about 20 words in German at Foundation tier and about 30 at Higher. You will hear each item **twice** in Section A and **three** times in Section B.

Section A

In Section A, these are some of the types of question you will hear:

- **Positive / Negative / Positive + Negative.** In this type of question, you will hear what people think about something. You write P if you think it is all positive; N if it is all negative; P + N if you think there is a mixture of both. Listen very carefully. You may hear **interessant** on the first hearing, but check what comes just before when you hear it for the second time. **Ich finde es interessant** is positive, but **ich finde es nicht interessant** is negative.
- **Choosing A, B or A + B.** You will hear someone speaking and you have to decide whether statement A, statement B or both A + B are correct. You may be sure that one of them is correct on the first hearing, but listen carefully on the second hearing to make sure the other statement isn't also correct.

Section B

In Section B, for the dictation, you will hear a number of short sentences in German. Usually there will be **four** sentences at Foundation tier and **five** at Higher. For each sentence, this is what happens:

- you hear the whole sentence.
- you hear the sentence broken up into two or three sections.
- you hear the whole sentence again.

If you hear it for the first time and there is something you miss, don't panic! You still have two chances to hear it again and get it right.

! **Remember:** At the end of the exam, you have 2 minutes to check your answers in the whole paper. This gives you a chance to look again at what you have written for the dictation and to spot any careless errors you may have made.

Speaking exam | Paper 2

The exam is divided into **three** sections which are the Role play; the Reading aloud of a text followed by four questions; the description of two Photo cards, followed by a conversation on the same theme as the photos. Below are some tips when you are aiming for full marks.

Role play

F Foundation | Full marks

- In order to get the full 10 marks, you will need to complete the five tasks by using a verb in each case. You will usually be asked to give an opinion. **Ich mag** (*I like*) is often a possible verb to use. For example, if the task is 'Give your opinion on means of transport in your area', you can say **Ich mag die Bahn**. If you have forgotten the word **Verkehrsmittel**, name one means of transport you know the German for: **Ich mag die Bahn**. This will get two marks.
- For one of the tasks, you will have to ask a question. This can sometimes look trickier than the others. Let's say the task is 'Ask your friend a question about their school'. There are many questions you could ask, but one of them would be to ask 'Do you like your school?' (**Magst du deine Schule?**)

H Higher | Full marks

- Look at the advice given for Foundation tier about the task where you have to ask a question. The question-asking task at Foundation and Higher tiers is very similar as regards the level of difficulty.
- The instructions say that you must use at least one verb in each task. Each task is worth 2 marks, whether one or two details are needed. You may also be asked to give one or two advantages or disadvantages in a task. Learn a selection of positive and negative adjectives for this kind of task. Positive ones include: **interessant** (*interesting*); **lustig** (*good fun*); **faszinierend** (*fascinating*); **einfach** (*easy*); **nützlich** (*useful*). Negative ones could be: **langweilig** (*boring*); **schwer** (*difficult*); **gefährlich** (*dangerous*); **nicht praktisch** (*useless*); **teuer** (*expensive*). If the task asks for two disadvantages of going to the cinema, you could say **Es ist langweilig und teuer** (even if you think it's fantastic!).

! **Remember:** In the Role play, always try to use language that you are confident you know the German for. The exam is not a time to make things up unless you really have to!

Reading aloud a text

- The main difference between Foundation and Higher tiers is the length of the text. There is a minimum of **35 words for Foundation** and **50 words for Higher**. There may be some words for both tiers that are longer ones. For example, German compound nouns such as **Lieblingsfach** have two or more words joined together. It is easier to break these compound nouns into smaller words to help you say them correctly.

Reading aloud a text continued

- Practise reading German aloud at home. If you get to a word that you are not sure how to pronounce, you can use a free online dictionary to help. Many of them include a function where by clicking **Hören** you can listen to the word being pronounced. Some of these also allow you to hear a word pronounced at half speed which can make things easier at first. You can also try typing *'pronounce ... in German'* on YouTube or Google. There are several sites that will pronounce the word for you. Try it with a tricky word like **langweilig** (*boring*). There will usually be more than one example. If one seems very fast, try another. AQA also have a pre-recorded sound bank of the complete vocabulary list available on their website.
- If there is an umlaut on a, o or u, it changes the pronunciation. So, to show how the German word **schön** is pronounced, it could be noted down as SHERN – which is different from **schon** (no umlaut) that you could note down as SHON.
- To get the full 5 marks for reading out the text, you don't have to be perfect. Concentrate on what you see as the trickiest words and note them down as suggested above. This will help you to make as few errors as possible and you may even be perfect!

! **Remember:** Take your time when reading the text. There are no extra marks for reading it quickly and, if you read it too quickly, you are more likely to mispronounce words.

Reading aloud a text – compulsory questions

After you have read the text, your teacher will ask you four questions. This is the case for both Foundation and Higher tiers, but the questions are slightly harder at Higher.

However, all questions at both tiers will be in the present tense and the mark scheme is the same for both tiers.

F Foundation and H Higher | Full marks

- To score full marks, you must answer all questions clearly.
- Two of your answers have to contain at least three verbs. For example:
  - **Was machst du auf deinem Handy?**
  - **Ich schicke Nachrichten, höre Musik und sehe Videos an.**
  (verbs underlined).
- One of your other answers must contain two verbs. For example:
  - **Wie findest du Dokumentarfilme?**
  - **Ich sehe nicht gern Dokumentarfilme, weil sie langweilig sind.**
  (verbs underlined).
- Your other answer can be as little as one word, provided it answers the question clearly. For example:
  - **Beschreib dein Handy.**
  - **Modern.**

Speaking exam continued

Description of the photos

F Foundation | Full marks

- Try to find 12 things or people in the photos that you definitely know the German for. List them by writing, for example: **Auf dem ersten Foto gibt es ein Mädchen, einen Junge und einen Hund.**

H Higher | Full marks

- Add as many other words as you can, to get about 15 or 16 bits of information in total.
- You can always say what is happening in the photos or what the people are doing, for example: **Das Wetter ist sonnig und die Jugendlichen spielen Fußball.**

Conversation

F Foundation | Full marks

- Wherever possible, give an extra piece of information when you answer a question and use a verb when you do. For example, your teacher asks you what you do with your friends: **Was machst du mit deinen Freunden?** You could talk about some of the places where you go: **Wir gehen ins Kino oder zum Park**. That is a good answer, but you only use one verb (**gehen**). If you can use more than one verb, do it! For example: **Wir gehen zum Park und wir spielen Fußball**.
- Vary what you say as much as you can and avoid repeating the same common language such as **ich mag**. You can always use **ich liebe** instead or adjectives that say why you might like something: **interessant, fantastisch, toll.**

H Higher | Full marks

- Try to answer most of the questions by using at least three verbs. There will be some occasions where you feel you can go beyond three. For example, you spend a lot of time on your mobile and your teacher asks you how you use technology: **Wie benutzt du Technologie?** You might think of quite a lot to say, using several verbs: **Ich benutze jeden Tag mein Handy, um mit Freunden zu reden. Gestern Abend habe ich meine Freundin angerufen und wir haben unsere Sommerpläne diskutiert. Es war schön.** Don't give very long answers too often, though.
- Your German should be mostly accurate and include a wide variety of different language with some more complex structures. Learn things like **wenn ich älter bin** (*when I'm older*); **ich habe gerade ... gesehen** (*I've just seen ...*); **ich lerne seit fünf Jahren Deutsch** (*I've been studying German for five years*); **wir sollten viel mehr machen, um ... zu ...** (*we should do much more in order to ...*).

Reading exam | Paper 3

In **Section A** of the exam, questions will either be multiple choice or they will need to be answered in **English**. In **Section B** you will translate some sentences from **German into English**. At Foundation tier, there will be about **35** words to translate and at Higher there will be about **50**.

F Foundation and H Higher | Full marks

Section A

In Section A, these are some of the types of question you will see:

- **Positive / Negative / Positive + Negative.** In this type of question, you will read what people think about something. You write P if you think it is all positive; N if it is all negative; P + N if you think there is a mixture of both. Read the text carefully. If you see the word **stressig**, just check whether it says, for example, **es ist stressig** (N) or **es ist nie stressig** (P).
- **Choosing A, B or A + B.** You will read a text and you have to decide whether statement A, statement B or both A + B are correct. You may be sure that one of them is correct, but read the rest of the text carefully to make sure the other statement isn't also correct.

Section B

In Section B you have to translate some German sentences into English. Don't leave any gaps. A guess always has a chance of being right; a gap doesn't. When you finish translating a sentence, read what you have written and make sure it makes sense. If it doesn't, there will be a mistake somewhere.

F Foundation | Full marks

Question 1

Find five things in the photo that you definitely know the German for and write five sentences all beginning with **Es gibt** (*there is/there are*), for example: **Es gibt eine Frau**. Each sentence you write is worth 2 marks.

If you can't find five things, you can always say what someone is doing, for example: **Die Frau geht joggen**; or you may be able to say what the weather is like if the photo is outside, for example: **Es ist sonnig**.

Question 2

You must write something that is clearly understandable about all five bullet points. You need to write about 50 words in total, which works out at around 10 words per bullet point. However, you can still get full marks if you write more about some of the bullet points than others.

Try to vary your language as much as you can, but it doesn't need to be complicated. For example, let's say one of the bullet points is **Das Essen**. You could write: **Ich esse gern Gemüse, weil sie gut für die Gesundheit sind. Ich hasse Pommes. Ich hasse** (*I hate*) is used instead of **Ich esse nicht gern** to avoid repeating the verb **esse**.

Question 3

For each question, look carefully at the three words you have to choose from. Verb endings and agreement of adjectives are always very important. For example: **Mein Vater trägt eine <u>braune</u> Hose** – *My dad is wearing <u>brown</u> trousers*. The word for 'wearing' is **trägt** and the adjective **braune** ends in an *'e'* because a feminine noun is being described.

Always write the word you have chosen in the space and be sure to spell the word correctly, including umlauts, or you will not get the mark.

Question 4 (translation)

When it is marked, the translation is divided into 15 sections. Each time you translate a section accurately enough to convey the meaning, you are given a tick. The ticks are added up and you get a mark out of 5 as follows: 13–15 ticks = 5 marks; 10–12 = 4; 7–9 = 3; 4–6 = 2; 1–3 = 1. There are a further 5 marks that are given for grammatical accuracy. The exam paper doesn't show what the 15 sections are.

Have a go at everything. If you leave any blanks because you don't know a word, you will lose marks. The examiner will have to assume that if you had given it a go, you would have got it wrong anyway, so you might as well try something.

As we saw in Question 3, verb endings and adjectives are important, so always check what you have written is absolutely clear. If you make a mistake and have to correct it, cross out the incorrect word and write the other one clearly. Don't write in very small handwriting to get the correct word into a small gap because it may not be clear enough for the examiner.

Question 5

You have two questions to choose from, but you should only answer one of them. Have a good look at the bullet points in each question before you start and think about which is the one where you feel most comfortable that you can write around **90** words in German.

To get full marks, you will have to give clear information about all three bullet points. This means that you will have to use three time frames to cover the present, past and future bullet points successfully.

You need to write around **90** words in total, which works out at about **30** words per bullet point. You won't be penalised if you write more on one bullet point than the others, but it is a good idea to have roughly the same number of words for each one. This is because you are asked to develop your ideas. For example, let's say that one bullet point asks you to write about what you do at the weekend. You could just write: **Am Wochenende gehe ich zum Park**. This is enough to cover the bullet point successfully. However, you would only be saying one thing. If you go on to write about **30** words, you will be developing your ideas, in other words writing more about what you do. Giving opinions is always a good way to develop what you write. This is what you could write: **Am Wochenende gehe ich mit Freunden zum Park. Wir spielen Fußball oder wir fahren Rad. Es macht viel Spaß. Manchmal besuche ich meine Großeltern und wir kochen zusammen. Es gefällt mir.**

For Assessment Objective 3 (AO3) you will need a good variety of vocabulary, so try not to repeat words wherever possible. Your writing should be as accurate as you can get it, but it doesn't have to be perfect. Vary your language, maybe by using expressions like these:

- **jedoch** – *however*
- **außerdem** – *besides, also* (a good alternative to **auch**)
- **anderseits** – *on the other hand*
- **der/die/das** – *who* (a good way to link separate phrases to make one longer sentence – **ich besuche meine Schwester, die in der Stadt wohnt**)
- **zum Beispiel** – *for example*

H Higher | Full marks

Question 1 (translation)

See the notes for Foundation Question 4. The requirements are the same at both tiers.

Question 2

See the notes for Foundation Question 5. The questions and mark scheme are identical at both tiers.

Question 3

There are 25 marks in total: 15 for Assessment Objective 2 (AO2), which is for writing around 150 words in clearly understandable German and for developing ideas and descriptions; 5 marks for AO3 range and use of language, which is for having a variety of vocabulary and grammatical structures and for being able to produce more complex language; 5 marks for AO3 accuracy, in other words the fewer mistakes you make, the better.

On AQA's website there is a copy of the mark scheme for the Higher, as well as the Foundation, papers. You will find examples of what is meant by development, variety of language and complex language. It is a good idea to look at this so you can see what examiners will be looking for.

You have two questions to choose from, but you should only answer one of them. Have a good look at the bullet points in each question before you start. Decide which one you feel most comfortable writing enough about to use around 150 words in German.

You need to write clear information in relation to both bullet points and develop your ideas and descriptions. Giving opinions and reasons is often a good way to do this.

There must be a very good variety of vocabulary, so try to impress by including as many different words as you can.

You must use complex language quite often. Remember you can see examples on AQA's website.

The two bullet points will refer to different time frames. Usually, one point will need you to answer in the present tense and the other will refer either to the past or to the future. Make sure you have used the correct tenses and endings for the verbs in each bullet point.

INDEX

NOTES, DOODLES AND EXAM DATES

67

Doodles

Exam dates

Listening: ....

Reading: ....

Speaking: ....

Writing: ....

EXAMINATION TIPS

When you practise examination questions, use the following tips collated from years of experience and examiner reports to help you maximise your result.

Written exams (Listening, Reading, Writing)

1. Ensure your handwriting is clear and legible.
2. Cross out any mistakes with one clear line.
3. Read the question instructions carefully.
4. **For Listening:**
   - Don't write answers while the recording is playing. Wait for the pause between the two recordings of a question or the pause between one question and the next.
   - In the dictation, you hear everything three times in total. Check your spellings when you hear each section.
5. **For Reading:**
   - Read forwards and backwards in a text from the key word in the question. Sometimes the answer comes after the key word and sometimes it comes before. Translate every word in the paragraph.
6. **For Listening and Reading:**
   - Look at the heading of the question. It is in English and gives you the question context, for example 'School'.
   - If you are asked to give a certain number of details, only give that number.
   - When answering with a letter, make sure the letter is written clearly. For example, the letter A can look like an H if you leave a gap at the top.
   - Don't leave any answers blank. A blank response will always score 0 but a guess may get a mark.
7. **For Writing:**
   - If a question asks you to write an approximate number of words, try to keep to roughly that number. If you write much more than that, you may make more errors and this can lead to a lower mark.
   - Mention all of the bullet points in an answer and tick them off on the question paper as you cover them.
   - Check that you don't miss out any parts of the translation.
   - Check your work carefully, especially verb tenses and endings.

Speaking exam

8. Use the 15 minutes of preparation time wisely. You can write notes for what you are going to say for the role play and for the description of the photos. For the reading aloud passage, you can write down tricky words as you will say them, for example *beziehung* as *bah-tzee-yung*.
9. You can ask for repetition of a question in any part of the test, but make sure you ask in German. You can say **Nochmal, bitte.**
10. Speak clearly at all times and don't read your notes from the preparation time too fast. There are no extra marks for speaking quickly.

Viel Glück!

New titles **coming soon!**

These guides are everything you need to ace your exams and beam with pride. Each topic is laid out in a beautifully illustrated format that is clear, approachable and as concise and simple as possible.

They have been expertly compiled and edited by subject specialists, highly experienced examiners, industry professionals and a good dollop of scientific research into what makes revision most effective. Past examination questions are essential to good preparation, improving understanding and confidence.

- Hundreds of marks worth of examination style questions
- Answers provided for all questions within the books
- Illustrated topics to improve memory and recall
- Specification references for every topic
- Examination tips and techniques
- Free Python solutions pack (CS Only)

Absolute clarity is the aim.

Explore the series and add to your collection at **www.clearrevise.com**

Available from all good book shops

amazon @pgonlinepub

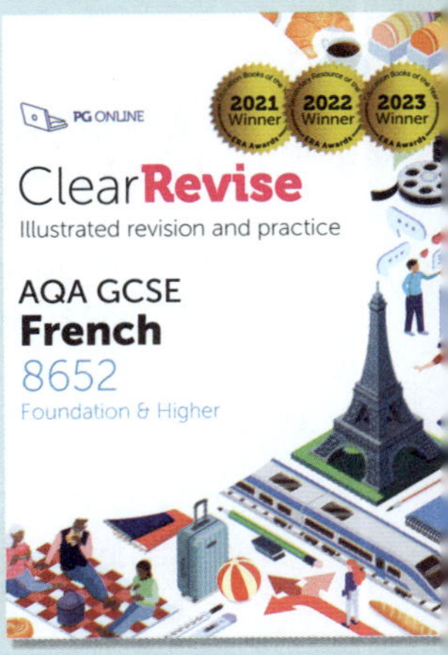

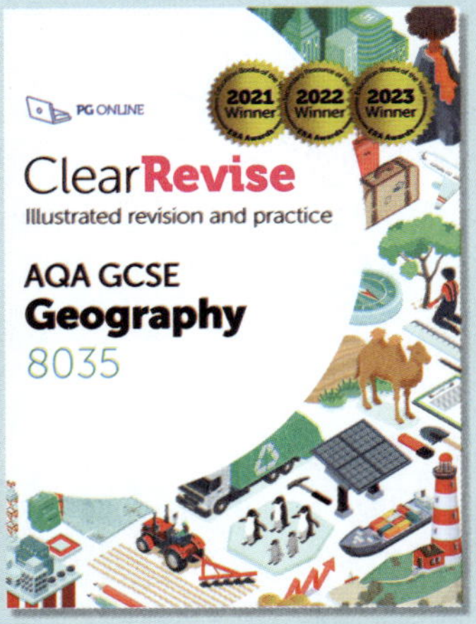